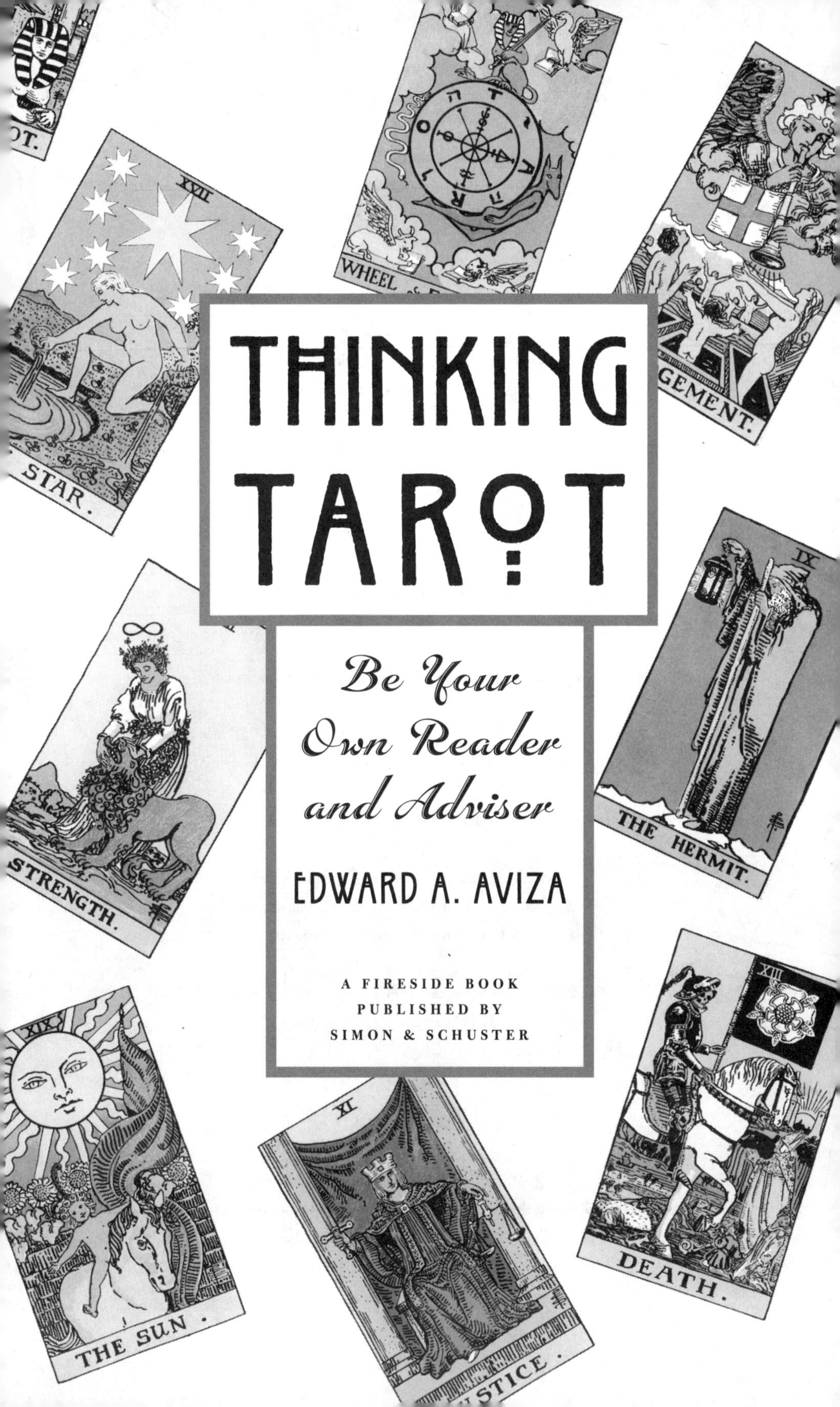

THINKING TAROT

Be Your Own Reader and Adviser

EDWARD A. AVIZA

A FIRESIDE BOOK
PUBLISHED BY
SIMON & SCHUSTER

FIRESIDE

Rockefeller Center

1230 Avenue of the Americas

New York, NY 10020

FIRESIDE and colophon are registered trademarks

of Simon & Schuster Inc.

DESIGNED BY DEBORAH KERNER

Manufactured in the United States of America

3   5   7   9   10   8   6   4   2

Library of Congress Cataloging-in-Publication Data

Aviza, Edward A.

Thinking tarot : be your own reader and adviser / Edward A. Aviza.

p.   cm.

Includes bibliographical references.

System requirements for accompanying computer disk:

386 or compatible CPU; highly recommend 486;

at least 4MB RAM; Windows version 3.1.

1. Tarot.   2. Tarot—Software.   3. CyberTarot (Computer file)   I. Title.

BF1879.T2A96   1997   <MRC>

133.3'2424—DC21   97-10329

CIP

ISBN 0-684-82274-1

This book and software package are dedicated to the memory of PATRICIA C. FLEMING and E. McCLUNG FLEMING, who first introduced the author to the beautiful symbols of the tarot in 1980. I'd like to thank you, Mac and Pat, for the inspiration and the teaching. I miss you both.

I'd also like to thank my wife, DALE AVIZA, for enduring my long days and nights at the computer, for her creative suggestions that improved both the book and the software, and for holding our lives together while I was working on this project.

ACKNOWLEDGMENTS

I would like to thank Seth Godin Productions for discovering my software and setting in motion the whole process that gave birth to this project. I'd also like to thank Karen Watts for discovering my writing. Without you, I'd still be coding away in oblivion.

CONTENTS

INTRODUCTION

Why Thinking Tarot and Cyber Tarot?

arot has been used and misused for centuries as both a means of divination and a tool for self-understanding. The images of tarot have often caused fear and superstition and to this day remain highly misunderstood. The purpose of *Thinking Tarot* and the CyberTarot software is to make the archetypal symbolism of the tarot available to a wider audience, and to utilize the images of tarot in a new, thoroughly modern medium. In attempting to reiterate the archetypes that shape our lives in the new idioms of the modern age, we hope to make the tarot useful to a large number of people who might not otherwise choose to work with these symbols. Tarot is not a cunning hoax but rather a collection of universal images that, when read with understanding and intuition, provide discernment into the human condition and connect us intimately with the history and struggles of humanity throughout the ages. Tarot is more a psychological tool than a mysterious fortune-telling game. Its power does not lie in some sort of inexplicable ability to see into the future but rather in its uncanny ability to help us see into ourselves.

The value of the tarot lies in the pictures and symbols that it uses to convey meaning, and in our interaction with those images. For centuries, cards have been the conventional medium used to display these images. However, the usefulness of the tarot is not limited to the specific medium of cardboard or paper; it is the *symbols* that are important, not the means used to present them. The advent of the personal computer as a tremendous cultural force provides an opportunity to interact with the tarot images in ways previously undreamed of. The fact that the computer is one of the most powerful communication tools in the late twentieth century can hardly be disputed. And though many feel threatened by the computer (as in the past many feared the advent of the printing press), it is but a *medium* of communication, as is a book, or a pack of cards. One interacts with all these media in a similar manner; we put our time and energy into understanding what we perceive, and in return receive knowledge that will equal or surpass the efforts we invest.

In CyberTarot you will see a mirror that reflects your own consciousness. Your interaction with the images on the screen will provide a means for obtaining insight into your own humanity. The tarot is a tool that helps us understand our motives and our inclinations. The images offer us the possibility of greater self-knowledge, and with this knowledge we come to an understanding of the questions we bring to the tarot. The answers you receive should be taken in this context and never interpreted as a predestined or fixed outcome to a question. Rather, the readings are a source of expression for your unconscious impulses and tendencies. Do not come to a reading expecting the cards to make decisions for you; the tarot can be used as a guide to understanding *yourself* but should never be looked to for sole direction on the decisions you must make. Your freedom as an individual is a key element in understanding the tarot. It is in the expression of this freedom that you come to know yourself more intimately, using the symbols of the tarot to enrich and further your spiritual growth.

Thinking Tarot was written to be a comprehensive and self-contained guide to using and understanding the tarot. However, the software included with this book offers you the opportunity to begin working with the tarot immediately, even before you begin to read the book in detail. You can install the software in a few minutes and do a complete tarot reading without any previous knowledge of how to work with the cards. The interface in CyberTarot is designed to be clear and intuitive, and the detailed on-line help system will assist you in quickly and easily working through a reading with the software. Of course, you may wish to work with real cards as well, and this book will prove to be a valuable guide to understanding their rich symbolism. The tarot will continue to offer its wisdom to you for years to come, and the more you learn of its magnificent symbology the more you will grow in the knowledge and understanding of yourself.

THINKING
TAROT

To install the software in your computer, first insert the enclosed CD-ROM into your CD drive. Then, from the Program Manager select **File,** then **Run** from the menu. If your CD drive is drive D:, type **D:\SETUP** into the **Command Line,** then click the **OK** button. If you are running Windows 95, you can open the **Control Panel** folder and double-click the **Add/Remove Programs** icon. Then click the **Install** button. Windows' Installation Wizard will guide you through the installation process.

When the installation begins, you will first see the **Initializing Setup** message box. After the initialization process, you may see another message with the following error: **Warning—cannot copy file D:\DDEML.DL_ since the destination file is already in use.** Simply click **OK** here, as this only means that you already have the required file available on your computer. Next, you will see a message box that says: **If you want to install CyberTarot in a different directory**

and/or drive, type the name of that directory. Install To: C:\TAROT. If you wish to install the software to a different location, type that location into the text box; otherwise click **Continue.** You'll have the choice of either a **Normal Installation,** which will require that you have the CD-ROM in the drive to use the software, or the **Fast Run** installation, which will install all files to your computer's hard disk. The installation process will take a few minutes, and when it is complete, a new Program Manager Group called **CyberTarot** will be created for you. To run the program, double-click the **CyberTarot** sun icon.

THINKING TAROT

How Does the Tarot Work?

The tarot is not magic or superstition, and its authority is not based in some occult or mysterious force. Rather, the power of the tarot comes from your own consciousness, from the thoughts and feelings that influence you and are important to you. The archetypical images of the tarot reflect the universal experience of humanity throughout the ages. In order to understand how the tarot works (that is, why it seems so accurate in describing a particular situation and predicting the way we will respond to that situation in the future), you must adopt a new understanding of the world and of your own mind. The underlying philosophy of the tarot is that everything in the universe is intimately connected. Because of this intimate connection among all things, an action in one place can have an effect, however subtle, upon everything else in the universe. The unconscious mind is a powerful force that creates our reality and influences everything with which we come into contact. The cards reflect our consciousness because of this interconnection to all things and because in each card we can see something of ourselves, regardless of what is happening in our lives. When we work with the images of the tarot, we interact directly with the universal images of archetypes and our personal energy influences the patterns that are revealed by the cards. This subtle interaction enables the tarot to reflect our situation and to offer us insight into our own personality and inclinations.

In understanding the tarot images that are revealed, it is important to remember that no interpretation is fixed and inflexible. The explanations of the cards in this book will attempt to guide you toward finding your own understanding of the significance of the cards, but they are not by any means the final word or even a complete explanation of the card meanings. What you bring to the images is far more important than what someone else might tell you is there. You must learn to think abstractly, in symbols, to glean the most value from the images of the tarot. Look carefully at the symbols, study the relationships of the cards in a spread, look beyond the explanations given. Try to see more than that which is obvious, ask yourself questions about the images, and let your imagination wander freely. There are no right or wrong ways to interpret the images, and what works for you may not work for someone else. The readings are a personal exploration of yourself, and the images are only keys to help you unlock the mysteries of your own spirit. The tarot should be used to help you develop your intuition, and it is only with a well-developed sense of intuition and self-knowledge that the archetypes depicted in the images will begin to bring light and understanding to your life.

The Archetypes

As the psychologist Carl Jung worked with his patients over the years, he noticed patterns of recurring images in their dreams and in their descriptions of the issues concerning them. Jung was, in addition to being a therapist, an avid scholar of religion, mythology, alchemy, and symbolism. He discerned many close correspondences between the images described by his patients and those found in the various mythological and religious traditions of the world. He also noticed that the same symbols were not only common to nearly all mythological systems but also occurred frequently in art forms such as poetry, painting, and sculpture. Jung coined the term *archetype* to describe these universal signs. In Jung's view, an archetype is a representation that has universal significance to all mankind because of its common applicability to all human experience. Jung, however, was not the first to notice the existence of such common themes in the consciousness of humanity. The archetypes as defined by Jung correspond very closely to Plato's idea of forms. Plato's forms are, however, linked directly to the manifestations of things in the world, in the sense of their being ontological prototypes of all existing things. Simply stated, this means that the forms have an independent existence somewhere in the universe, and they act as the formative images or templates upon which specific items in the world are modeled. The form of a chair, for example, is the preexisting model of all chairs that exist in the material world.

Jung's archetypes are not necessarily self-existent prototypes of the things that exist in the world; rather they are conceptual prototypes that exist primarily in the consciousness and psychology of humanity. In other words, these archetypes really only exist in the human psyche, yet they are common in experience to all human beings. To explain the common ground in which these archetypes are found, Jung hypothesized the presence of a collective unconscious, which links the subconscious minds of all individual human beings. This collective unconscious may also be referred to as the universal mind, or shared mind, to which all people have access, although in most cases only indirectly, through symbols, dreams, or through fortuitous events, commonly known as meaningful coincidences. Jung coined the term *synchronicity* to refer to these kinds of events.

Synchronicity

Synchronicity is the occurrence of incidents that appear to be related to each other in some way but for which there is no apparent causal relationship. Normally, we consider causality when we think about the interrelationship of events: I push a boulder over a hill, the boulder rolls down the hill and splashes into the ocean. The causes of each event (the initial push, the boulder rolling, the splash of the water) are clear and obvious. The relationship between synchronistic events, however, is not at all so clear. As a simple example of synchronicity, consider the following scenario: You are walking along a street and suddenly start thinking of an old school friend whom you haven't seen or thought of in years, and then a few hours later that person happens to call you on the phone and you have a wonderful, uplifting conversation. Did your thinking about that person somehow cause him to think of you and then call you? Are these two events completely unrelated, or is there some unknown reason you both began to think of each other at the same time? When you consider the "coincidence" later, does some sort of meaning begin to appear? You may realize, for example, that the conversation you had with your old friend was *exactly* what you needed at just that time.

The collective unconscious not only provides a "synchronistic bridge" that links all human beings to each other, but also provides each individual with access to the universal store of archetypes that contain all human memory, experience, and conceptualization from time immemorial. Common archetypes include universal concepts such as motherhood and fatherhood in the broadest meanings of those terms, as well as specific images from our experience such as the sun, the moon, and the earth. Other archetypes are more abstract and include concepts such as numbers and shapes. The number two, for example, often represents tension or conflict but may also represent unity and the peaceful coexistence of opposites. The circle is a powerful archetype that represents fulfillment, completion, and the cyclical nature of time. These archetypal images are expressed and shared among peoples through myths, religious expression, artistic creations, symbolism, dreams, and intentional "synchronistic tools" such as the tarot.

To call the tarot a synchronistic tool implies that the images portrayed on the cards can provide a connection to the collective unconscious that ordinarily remains out of our grasp. This book's perspective on the tarot is that its primary purpose is to serve as a tool for the exploration of the collective unconscious, the inner mind of which we are normally unaware. We are too distracted, too busy with our external affairs to find the solitude and quiet peace in which to explore our inner depths. To work with the tarot successfully requires a good deal of effort and concentration, and as much freedom from the distractions of the daily routine as possible. Your ideal situation for exploring the tarot will be as different from that of someone else as your interpretations and impressions of the images are. It will take time to become intimate with the symbolism of the cards; it will take energy and effort to be able to interpret their meanings and understand the depths of wisdom they express. But once you become familiar enough with the images to be able to "think" their symbols, you will have mastered the mysteries they represent, which are really the mysteries of your own mind.

How to "Think" Tarot

The only way to gain fluency in a foreign language is to learn to *think* in that language. Language instructors urge their students to stop mentally translating from their own language to the new language because the translation process hinders a true grasp of the new language and prevents fluency. The act of translating is indicative of the learning process in that translation is required only until the language is actually mastered by the student. Once the student has internalized the language, there is no longer a need for translation. She has become familiar enough with the language to be able to think in that language. The ability to think in a particular language creates the possibility of effective communication; the individual can comprehend its representations clearly and express herself effectively with its spoken and written forms.

Symbols, as we have seen, are expressions of the archetypes that are shared among all peoples. According to A. E. Waite, the designer of the Rider-Waite deck, the images of the tarot are a kind of language of symbolism. We could just as easily call them a language of the archetypes, using Jung's terminology. Individuals newly exposed to the symbols comprised in this language require continual translation in order to understand them, just as an individual unfamiliar with French requires translation in order to understand it. Translations of the language of tarot are typically done either by tarot readers who act as live interpreters of the messages contained in the tarot language, or by reference to books or other media aids such as instructional videos or software. Tarot readers must be able to comprehend immediately at least a minimum of the symbolism that makes up the language if they are to provide any value to their clients; they must have enough facility with this arcane language to translate its meanings without resorting to other aids such as books or dictionaries of symbols. The ability of readers to translate the images of the tarot into comprehensible and coherent messages for their clients is usually based on years of experience. Translation skills are not exclusive to people with psychic or other paranormal abilities, however. Rather, a reader's skill is based on the development of intimacy with the card images through extensive exposure to them, and on the development of personal intuition. Anyone who is willing to put forth the effort to learn the language of symbols can learn to read the tarot effectively.

Words and Phrases: The Basic Elements of Language

The first steps in learning a new language require the student to learn some basic words, phrases, and elements of syntax. In the tarot, the "words" correspond to the individual symbolic elements displayed on a particular card. For example, the card of the Sun offers a number of interesting symbolic elements that contain rich meaning in and of themselves. Most visibly, the large, anthropomorphic (human-faced) sun at the top of the card represents the archetypal form of life in its broadest and most encompassing sense. The sun can also represent the inner light of the human spirit, or the divine light of God. The white horse typically represents purity because of its unblemished white color, and power because of the obvious strength of the animal. In addition, the white horse may represent the unconscious mind or the spirit of a person. This card depicts a smiling, playful child riding the horse. Symbolically, a child represents innocence, purity, and perhaps naïveté and lack of experience. A child is open to the world around him and is willing to embrace it joyfully until his experience tempers his openness with caution, skepticism, and possibly even fear. This childlike openness is represented by the wide-open arms of the child in our image. The child carries an enormous red banner in his left hand. Red is often considered a color of warning or danger. Yet it can also be a symbol of life; blood is a red substance that carries the life-sustaining elements of nourishment throughout our bodies. Fire, which brings heat and light, is also red. The banner is a symbol of victory in the conquest of opposing forces. In the background behind the

25

child, there is a walled garden filled with sunflowers. The garden can be considered an archetype corresponding to the human soul. In this case, the garden is teeming with lush plant life; the sunflowers symbolize fruitfulness and a plentiful harvest of bread for now and seeds for the future. Each individual card in the tarot deck is, like that of the Sun, replete with a collection of rich symbolic images that offer abundant possibilities for interpretation.

However, each tarot card is not simply a collection of random or unrelated symbols waiting to be interpreted one by one. An individual card, taken as a complete unit, can be considered a "phrase" in our language analogy. The power, therefore, of individual symbolic elements on a particular card is enhanced or diminished by its relationship to the other symbols depicted on that card. So again, in our Sun card example, we can analyze the total collection of images to extrapolate a richer meaning overall than if we were to examine only the individual symbol elements themselves. Taken together, we have the following collection of words or symbol elements: 1) a human-faced sun; 2) a young, innocent child; 3) a white horse; 4) a walled garden; 5) an abundant crop of sunflowers, and 6) a large red banner. What do these images have to do with each other? How, if at all, are they related?

To begin our analysis, we should start in very broad terms by first examining the overall mood or theme of each symbol on the card. In the case of the Sun, the symbol elements primarily reflect the archetypal concepts of light, innocence, victory, joy, and fruitfulness. These concepts are related to the experience of spirituality. In nearly all of the world's religions, the desire of an individual soul for union with the divine forms the basis for mysticism, prayer, and in fact all spiritual practice. Taken as a whole, then, the Sun refers to the spiritual victory of an individual soul in attempting to attain union with God. But there are two images that may conflict with this overall theme: the walled garden and the red banner. A wall could symbolically represent a blockage of spiritual progress, or a place of imprisonment, separation, or confinement. The color red might be a sign of warning, a red flag in the very literal sense! If we look closely at the card, we see that the child appears to be riding out of the garden. If, as mentioned above, the walled garden is an image of the individual soul, then why would the child, who here appears to represent the soul as well, be riding out of it?

In the mystical traditions, the soul that seeks union with God must be willing to die and be reborn: "Unless the grain of wheat should fall to the ground and die, it shall not bring forth fruit." An enclosed garden represents an encapsulated soul, meaning a soul that is wrapped up in its own ego and considers itself a completely separate entity from the rest of the universe. The person who is enthralled with her personal preoccupations is unable to experience the divine union because the walled garden is carefully protected by the ego's desire to preserve itself; the person's attention is focused on shoring up the wall itself and digging around in the dirt! However, the spirit of the individual willing to put aside his own need to build up and preserve the wall is able to look up to the healing light of the sun (the divine spirit) and receive its enrichment; just as a garden requires light and nurturing to thrive, so does the human spirit require the light of God, and the inner light of a pure spirit. The child rides out of the garden because the spirit represented in the card has been reborn by allowing the spirit of God to enter it; the wall is no longer an insurmountable obstacle.

Our "phrase" then might be this: The sun (divine spirit) shining into the walled garden (individual soul) produces the abundant fruit of creativity, imagination, and spiritual awareness (the sunflowers). The soul is then freed from the constraints of its own ego limitations and returned to the innocence of a pure spirit. (The child rides out of the garden, the walls are no longer a barrier.) The pure spirit is a source of power and strength (the white horse) in that it receives nour-ishment directly from the source of life itself (the sun). The red flag would, in view of this overall interpretation, most likely be a banner of power and the victory of the soul over its former constraints. If it is to serve as a warning of any sort, it may simply be a message not to look back once the experience of spiritual freedom is attained.

Sentences and Paragraphs

To continue with our linguistic analysis, we need to begin forming "sentences and paragraphs" with the "words and phrases" of our card images. In the tarot, the sentences are constructed by putting collec-tions of cards together in specific patterns called spreads or layouts that help us with interpretation. Later in this book, you will find a col-lection of spreads you can use to read the tarot, but there are literally countless spreads possible. You can even create your own spreads by adapting existing ones to your own preference, or by using a particular symbol, symbolic shape, or number as the basis for a new spread. A spread is nothing more than a framework or method for creating a complete symbolic statement using the tarot images. The process of reading the tarot can be done using a number of different methods. You can, for example, select the cards you want and create your own reading to explore a particular issue that is of concern to you. To work with the tarot in this way requires some familiarity with its language so you can select appropriate cards and position them in such a way that their interrelationship helps you find new ways of understanding the current issue. Another more typical way to work with the tarot is to se-lect the cards at random. Usually, to allow the tarot symbols to speak their meanings to us, the cards are arranged into a spread blindly, meaning that you don't actually see the specific cards as you select them and lay them into their respective positions.

The process of using a spread to do a tarot reading is simple and straightforward, and the CyberTarot software is designed to get you started right away. First, think of a question you want the tarot images to help you understand more clearly. Then, shuffle the deck of cards while you are thinking of your question until you feel a sense that the cards are ready to speak to you. This feeling is not necessarily a blinding realization that the answer is at hand; rather it is a quiet intuition, a sense, or a hunch that you and the cards are ready to communicate. If this intuition is difficult to perceive at first, don't worry! It may take some practice with the cards to get in tune with your own intuitive powers, but with a little effort anyone can become a good reader.

When you feel ready to deal the cards, you can either start immediately, or you may cut the cards first and then deal. The process of shuffling is of primary importance because that is when you are most directly influencing and interacting with the cards. Cutting the deck— some books are very specific on this, requiring, for example, that you cut the deck only with your left hand and in a left-to-right direction!— may or may not be useful in producing an effective reading, but you can decide if you feel it's necessary to cut the cards when doing a reading. If you're working with the software, you won't be able to cut the cards, but you can shuffle them as long as you like. Select cards one by one and place them in positions that correspond to the spread you are using. In CyberTarot you simply drag the cards you want to select into the "pit" at the bottom of the screen, and they will automatically be placed into their correct positions.

At least initially, the primary spread to use is the Celtic Cross because it is probably the most common and easily comprehensible to work with. When working with actual cards, you can either place the cards faceup, or you can place them facedown and turn them over either one at a time or all at once. It is usually effective to turn the cards over one at a time and then analyze them individually in relation to their current position in the spread and in relation to other cards that may be visible. The software allows you to reveal cards one at a time, or all at once. Once all the cards have been turned over, you are ready to begin your interpretation.

The method of understanding the sentences and paragraphs of a complete tarot reading is similar to that of putting the words of individual symbols together into the phrases of complete card images. Each position in a spread contains, by convention, a certain significance to which the meaning of the card occupying that position must be applied. Just as the combination of individual symbolic elements on a particular card must be considered as a complete unit to understand the total significance of that card, so must a full spread be interpreted as a complete package of meaning composed of "words, phrases, sentences, and paragraphs" that together form a unified message. In all cases, the specific meaning of a complete spread depends not so much on the actual cards drawn as upon your current state of life and your intuition about how the language of the cards is speaking directly to you. The reading process is very subjective in that the same spread would mean different things to different people, depending on their own life situations. The purpose of laying out the cards is that of stimulating your imagination and intuition, and prompting you to look inward to examine your own life.

A Sample Reading

The best way to become familiar with reading a spread is to actually do it, so let's run through a hypothetical reading and interpretation using the Celtic Cross spread. This sample reading is offered to give you a start in learning to translate the language of the tarot. You can work with this sample by using the **Create Reading** feature of the CyberTarot software. Complete interpretations for all seventy-eight tarot cards, as well as detailed information on a variety of spreads you can use, are covered in later sections of this book. The language analogy (comparing the tarot symbols to words, phrases, sentences, and paragraphs) will be carried on throughout the rest of the book and in the section of card interpretations.

For our example, let's assume the question is, "How will my financial situation influence or affect my spiritual life?" We would begin by shuffling and dealing the cards. Then, we would turn over the cards one by one (or all at once, if you prefer). Our hypothetical reading has the layout shown on the next page.

Card One: THE SUN
Card Two: THE FOUR OF PENTACLES
Card Three: THE TWO OF SWORDS
Card Four: THE TOWER
Card Five: THE FOUR OF CUPS
Card Six: THE EMPRESS
Card Seven: THE FOUR OF WANDS
Card Eight: THE SEVEN OF SWORDS
Card Nine: THE SIX OF WANDS
Card Ten: THE EIGHT OF PENTACLES

If the Sun is drawn as the first card (the significator, which represents you at the present time), the meaning implied may be that there is a growing awareness of spirituality in your life, or that you are in a positive state of mind in general. The connection between the imagery of the Sun and the position of the significator should act as a stimulant to your intuition in regard to your current situation. For example, if you are *not* in a positive psychological or spiritual state, you might need to ask yourself why. The Sun in such a case might indicate the need to look inward to determine the causes of your current state of mental and spiritual health. The simple fact of the Sun being drawn as the significator cannot be interpreted universally in the same way, but rather must be understood in the context of your individual circumstances.

The second card drawn in the Celtic Cross spread is known as the crossing card. This card position represents current influences on you, which may be positive or negative, depending upon the image drawn and your own situation. If the crossing card drawn over the Sun is, for instance, the Four of Pentacles, the indication may be that your psychological and spiritual health is being affected in some way by your concerns about, or relationship to, money or material things in general, since the suit of pentacles suggests temporal rather than spiritual issues. If your current attitude is joyful and positive, then the combination of the Sun crossed by the Four of Pentacles could indicate in part that your current joy might be positively affected, either by financial prosperity in your life or by your own psychological detachment from overwhelming worry and concern about money. However, if the Sun is more of a challenge to you because your current state of mind is negative, then the combination of the cards in these positions may indicate that you are unhappy either because you are lacking financial or material resources, or because you are overly attached to material things or concerned about them to an unhealthy extreme. You may, in fact, be quite prosperous and wealthy, but if your psychological attachment to wealth and material possessions is a burden because it causes excessive worry and stress, then you may need to explore methods of changing your perspective or your relationship to the material world. The message might be that you need to relax and not worry so much, or that you need to develop a more active spiritual life. Again, the point to keep in mind is that the cards and their interpretations are to be used as points of departure for a deeper examination of yourself. The symbols are links to your own unconscious, which is connected to the collective unconscious. The messages offered by the tarot need to be thoughtfully considered and weighed in light of your own inner state of being.

For the third card, we have drawn the Two of Swords. The third position in the Celtic Cross spread represents the foundation or root issue at the heart of your question. The Two of Swords contains the general indication of a choice that must be made but that we may be avoiding because of the difficulty of the choice. There is a strong aspect of duality to this card, which often indicates conflict between opposing forces, desires, or influences. In our spread, we can see a possible conflict in the interaction between the Sun, representing spirituality, and the Four of Pentacles, representing attachment to the material world. The root issue that has drawn us to the cards appears in this case to be a sense of conflict between our spiritual and material natures. However, a more positive interpretation of this card as the foundation may be that we have already achieved a healthy balance between our inner and outer realities. The number two does not necessarily always represent tension between the opposites, but may in fact indicate a proper balance between those opposites. Again, the specific interpretation depends more than anything else on your own intuition and awareness of your current state of mind.

The fourth card in the Celtic Cross spread represents past events, issues, and concerns. This card denotes a situation that is passing, or has already passed, out of your life. In our example this card is the Tower, an image that at first glance appears to be quite difficult to deal with. The card depicts the destruction of an enormous castle and the fall of its inhabitants to the depths below. Since this card appears in the position representing the past, there is a strong indication of the destruction of some psychological edifice by which we had previously been controlled or hindered. The Tower may, in our spread, indicate that you had experienced a long struggle to break free of an over-whelming attachment to money or material things. The Sun, as the significator in our spread, then augurs a new dawning in your con-sciousness of spiritual awareness or at least a more balanced perspec-tive on the things of this world. The powerful edifice of worldly attachment may at last be crumbling in the dawning awareness of the more important things in life. The structure of our reading thus far in-dicates that you are likely to be undergoing a period of transition from an old way of being to a new way, one that may be more in tune with your deeper consciousness, and one that will more than likely increase your sense of joy and well-being in the long term.

The fifth position in the Celtic Cross spread is known as the crown, and represents issues that are of importance to you now and that may affect you in the future. The crown is a bridge between the present and the future, and as such it not only indicates current pat-terns of consciousness but also augurs potential future influences. In our spread, we have drawn the Four of Cups. At first glance, the card very clearly reflects the issue of choice and self-determination indi-cated by the Two of Swords, which appeared as our foundation. The young man sitting under the tree is faced with a choice among four ap-parently identical cups. When faced with a difficult decision, we often have a terrible time trying to weigh the pros and cons of the options be-fore us and sort out the consequences of each. The only true answer must come from within the deepest part of one's own spirit, in the heart of hearts where the spirit of God dwells. The young man in our image seems to be looking away from all the cups, as though he were lost in the contemplation of his own thoughts and feelings; he is look-ing inward for guidance, rather than trying to find it outside of himself.

This card confirms much in our reading so far, and is a perfect crown for all that has already been revealed. In a few broad strokes, we see that there is a creative tension of some sort between the desire for the spirit and the desire for the material. The Sun indicates that the truth is to be found only within the walled garden of our own soul nourished by the power of the divine, despite any outside influences. The choice must be made blindly, in a sense, because the full conse-quences of our actions can never be fully known in advance. Thus, the woman in our foundation card (the Two of Swords) wears a blindfold, signifying the difficulty of the decision. But we have made great progress by breaking through certain barriers that hindered us in the past, and now we are, like the Buddha, sitting under the Tree of En-lightenment (the Axis Mundi or World-Navel) in the transition be-tween the present and the future. The choice here is not necessarily to reject either the spiritual or the material at the expense of the other, but perhaps it is simply a question of how to express a proper equilibrium between these important and complementary aspects of ourselves.

The sixth card of the Celtic Cross spread more clearly de-notes the influences that are likely to affect you in the future. It is very important here not to consider this card (or the full reading, for that matter) as a guide on which to base your decisions, or as a sign of a fixed and predetermined outcome. The influences in one's future can often be determined rather quickly by observing patterns in one's past and present. This card more strongly represents the likely flow of cir-cumstances in one's life based on what has already come to pass.

A meteorologist can make predictions for future weather pat-terns on the basis of past and current movements in wind directions, cloud masses, and pressure systems. Nonetheless, despite the fact that all current indications point, for example, toward a storm in your city tomorrow, you may have a beautiful sunny day instead. The tarot can indicate possible future patterns based on the psychological momentum you have created thus far, but it is always within your power to alter the course of future events.

In our reading, the Empress appears as the harbinger of future conditions. The Empress is a card of copious fruitfulness, joy, and fulfillment. We can immediately see a link between this card and our significator, the Sun. Both cards contain indications of positive trends, and the fact that both the significator and the future positions contain this general mood is a sign that the changes we may be experiencing are likely to continue for the positive if we maintain our current direction. The choices we are faced with in the foundation and the crown are, of course, very much able to alter this positive course, but because the significator carries such a powerful indication of positive energies, we are very likely to continue in this trend.

The seventh card in the Celtic Cross spread corresponds to your emotional state at the time of the reading. This card is very closely associated with the significator in that it complements and enhances the meaning of the first card. The combination of the significator and the card of feelings and emotions offers an intimate picture of your current inner life; together they present a snapshot of your overall psychological state at the time of the reading. In our example spread, we have drawn the Four of Wands in this position. The number four symbolically represents stability, completion, and realization. The Four of Wands depicts the celebration of a wedding, which is complemented by the richness of flower bouquets, a canopy of lush greenery, and the castle in the background. The connection between this card and our significator, the Sun, is again quite clear. The recurring appearance in this spread of propitious images seems to confirm that our positive state of mind in the present is likely to continue into the future. Another potent connection to notice here is the one between the Four of Pentacles as our crossing card, and the Four of Wands as our card of emotions. Both cards contain the symbolism of the number four, representing stability in a general sense. The Pentacles represent money or the material world, whereas the Wands represent fire, creativity, and spirituality. One way to interpret the occurrence of the Four of Wands in the position of emotions is that the marriage represented in the card corresponds to the union of the apparently opposing forces of the significator and the crossing card. Thus far, then, our reading indicates that a process of working out an appropriate balance between the inner life of the spirit and the outer life of the world is a preeminent concern and is probably the focus of much of your psychological energy.

The eighth card in our spread represents the influence or actions of other people in your life. This influence may be direct or indirect, and may even denote what you think others think of you! In our spread, the Seven of Swords appears in this position. At first glance, this card offers a paradox. The character in the card appears to be a thief stealing a cache of swords from the military camp in the background, yet he is smiling and seems to be mocking his victims from a distance. His action contains a good deal of negative energy, yet he looks as if he's experiencing pleasure from the experience. Although a tarot reading should not be taken literally or at face value, we nevertheless can sense a bit of tension in our reading because of this card. The indication, however, is not necessarily that someone is "out to get you" or plotting to steal from you in the literal sense. This card, in the entire context of our reading, may point to the need to be aware of the potential of damaging influences from others in our lives. All too often we allow the opinions or words of others to dampen our spirits or affect our decisions despite our better judgment.

Perhaps the message of this card in our reading is that we must remain centered within our own "walled garden" of the soul, which is nourished directly by the source of life itself. If we are easily swayed by worry over other people's opinions of us, we will never be at peace, simply because our relationships with others vary so greatly in their nature.

The ninth card in the Celtic Cross spread denotes our hopes, dreams, and desires for the outcome of the issue we have brought to the tarot. In this position we find the Six of Wands, a card with very strong indications of victory, success, and fulfillment. In light of the rest of our reading, this card clearly indicates that we have a great desire for a successful outcome of the issues and choices facing us in the present. The victorious rider in this card is closely linked with the Tower of card number four. In our recent past, according to the card in this position, we struggled with and overcame a barrier to our growth. Now, in the card representing our hopes, we express the desire to continue victoriously against the difficulties and challenges we faced before. In addition, this card is symbolically very similar to the Sun, our significator, in that the child riding out of the garden is representative of a spiritual liberation that comes as the result of opening ourselves to receive the nourishment of the divine. Both cards contain elemental imagery relating to victory, achievement, and fulfillment. Apparently (and not surprisingly!) our hope for the outcome of the issue at hand is simply that we continue in a positive and creative direction.

The tenth and final card of the Celtic Cross spread represents the final outcome or resolution of the reading. Again, be careful in your readings not to interpret the results of a spread literally; the culmination represented by the final card should be understood as a final complement to the entire reading that can clarify issues or questions remaining from the rest of the reading.

In our spread, the Eight of Pentacles is drawn as the final card. Interestingly, the image of Pentacles appearing here at the conclusion is directly related to the crossing card, which indicated a potential imbalance in terms of our interaction with money or the material world in general. The eight is not only the double of the four, which represents stability, but is also a number signifying spirituality and renewal. The eight displayed sideways is known as the lemniscate, which is a symbol for eternity, higher consciousness, divinity, and spirituality. The Eight of Pentacles, as our culminating card, seems to indicate the final union of the opposites (the *coniunctio oppositorum* of which Jung wrote) represented in our significator and crossing card combination.

The imagery of the card also indicates a more balanced perspective on money than seems to be present in the image of the Four of Pentacles. Our crossing card contained the possible implication of an unhealthy attachment to material things. Our culminating card signifies the need not only to work for our material rewards (the obvious image of the man working on one of the pentacles) but also to continue the work of the spirit (suggested by the number eight) in keeping the balance from tipping to one or the other extreme. The sense of psychological symmetry in the creative tension between, and the ultimate union of, presumably opposing forces (which appeared so frequently in our spread) is confirmed by our final card.

The sample reading given here, although apparently complex and detailed, only begins to scratch the surface of the depths of meaning, the limitless possibilities of interpretation present in a typical tarot layout. But the process of reading the cards is done in just this way; to get full value from a spread of cards, you must spend time absorbing the language of the images, comparing the individual symbolic elements ("words") in each card with other elements on that card, as well as with the symbolic elements of the other cards in the spread. Then you must consider each card individually, as a complete "phrase" of meaning, and examine its meaning in light of the position in which it appears in the spread.

In addition to exploring the cards themselves and the conventional meanings implied in the positions of the spread, you must also consider the meanings of numerical values, not only in terms of the ordinal position of a card in the spread, but also its own implicit numerical value. You must carefully consider the relationships among the cards in the spread: Each position complements and clarifies the meanings of the other positions in the spread. Any card appearing in any position may find a powerful counterpart in any other card appearing in any other position, and these relationships must all be carefully considered.

The primary exercise in working with the tarot is to attempt to look beyond the obvious in the meanings of the cards. For example, in the Empress you may have seen a powerful connection with the archetypal image of motherhood or, more broadly, parenthood or nurturing. This may indicate a connection between your current concerns about your financial situation and the attitudes you developed about money from your family. These meanings must be explored in the context of your subjective reality and the current circumstances of your life, your psyche, and your spiritual condition. Explore the various relationships in the spread and use your imagination and intuition to feel the links in meaning that will allow the spread to speak its meaning to you. When read with care, diligent effort, and a watchful imagination, the tarot can be an excellent tool for personal growth and increased self-awareness. If you take the time to examine your tarot spread as a complete statement, a collection of words, phrases, sentences, and paragraphs that together offer insight and understanding into your own life, you will be richly rewarded with a more highly developed sense of intuition, a keener imagination, and a spirit more deeply in communion with itself.

The Meaning of Reversed Cards

A subject of great debate among tarot readers is the use and meaning of reversed or upside-down cards. Typically, when a reader shuffles a deck of cards and lays them out in a spread, a few cards will turn up reversed. This, of course, depends on the shuffling technique, as well as the physical method of laying the cards down in a spread, and whether the deck is kept neatly arranged in a "right-side-up" manner. Many tarot experts consider that the appearance of a reversed card in a spread alters its meaning. Usually, this difference is a subtle reversal. So, for example, if you draw the Three of Swords right side up, it may be an indication of difficulties in the area of romance and relationships. However, if you draw this card reversed, it may be the very opposite indication of success and happiness in relationships. Similarly, if you draw the Sun right side up, the meanings are clearly very positive and joyful. However, if you draw the Sun reversed, there may be a need to temper the positive aspects of the Sun with caution and an awareness of possible difficulties even in the midst of joyous times.

The opposing position with regard to reversed cards is that the card interpretations are not significantly altered by their appearance. The general perspective to have about reversed cards is simply that they may indicate a subtle transformation of the meaning of the card, although this is not necessarily the case. As the individual approaching the tarot for understanding of your important issues, you must decide whether or not you feel there is any significance in the appearance of a reversed card. For the sake of clarity, separate interpretations for reversed cards have not been included in this book. However, the CyberTarot software allows you to use reversed cards if you like. If you decide not to use reversed cards, you can disable this feature by unchecking the box that reads **Use Reversed Cards** on the **Setup Screen.**

In a reading with actual cards, many readers simply turn over any reversed cards that appear because they don't necessarily ascribe any special significance to the appearance of a reversed image. Reversed cards may also cause confusion for individuals who are new to reading the tarot. Each card in itself contains positive and negative aspects, just as our consciousness contains elements of light and darkness. You must determine in the context of your own work with the tarot whether reversed cards present you with a different perspective on your readings or give additional richness to the interpretations you seek.

The Structure and Design of the Tarot Deck

The modern tarot deck, as it has evolved over the centuries, is generally thought to be a composite of two originally separate decks that were in widespread use during the late Middle Ages and early Renaissance. These two parts, now unified into one deck (typically seventy-eight cards, although some decks vary), remain conceptually separate in a number of ways. Historically, the subset of the tarot deck known as the major arcana (also called the trump cards) was the only part of the deck with full illustrations depicting symbolic meanings on the cards. The other primary subset of the deck is known as the minor arcana (often called the pip cards), which historically only depicted numbers and the suit symbols. The minor arcana cards are the predecessors of our modern playing cards and were originally used primarily for games of chance. The pips were also occasionally used for fortune-telling, with their primary symbolic meanings gleaned from numerological analysis of their face values combined with the general meanings of the suit symbols. The analysis of the minor arcana cards was greatly augmented in the Rider-Waite deck by the inclusion of detailed images for each card. These images expanded the basic significance of each card inherent in the combination of its suit and numerological meanings. As these games evolved over the centuries they were ultimately merged together to become the larger tarot deck we are familiar with today. Although the trumps gradually fell out of widespread use as a game on their own, the pip cards evolved separately into the modern fifty-two-card deck that is primarily used for contemporary card-based games. In time, the combined deck that evolved into the tarot came to be used more and more as a tool for divination and less as a gaming device.

The four suits of the minor arcana correspond to the four suits of modern playing cards: wands to diamonds, cups to hearts, swords to spades, and pentacles to clubs. Each suit contains one ace, nine numbered cards from two to ten, and four court cards, which include pages (or squires), knights, queens, and kings. In our modern playing card decks, the knights have disappeared and the pages have become jacks. The fifty-six cards of the minor arcana were given symbolic pictures for the first time in the Rider-Waite tarot deck. However, the court cards always held additional significance among the pips because they depict people in various social states, representing hierarchical rank or status. The court cards are often considered keys to personality types in readings of the tarot, and they are very powerful images for self-exploration. The court cards are also thought to act as a symbolic bridge between the minor arcana and the major arcana because of the additional imagery they contain, which expanded their divinatory meaning.

The suit symbols themselves represent various emotional or psychological states as well as other archetypal meanings. For example, they also correspond to the four primary elements long held to be the basic components of the universe (fire, water, air, and earth). The wands in general represent fire, creativity, and the life force that animates matter. In the Rider-Waite deck, the wands are always depicted in the early stages of blossoming, indicating a strong sense of potentiality, creativity, and the renewal of life. Taking this into account, we can see how an image like the Ace of Wands would represent the beginnings of new life, new creative projects, or the beginnings of an adventure. The cups correspond to water and represent matters of the heart and the emotions in general. Cups are passive and receptive by nature, with their purpose lying in the potential to be filled with water or some other substance. The Ace of Cups therefore might represent the be-

ginnings of a new relationship, or the dawning of a new spiritual awareness in one's life. The swords embody the qualities of the element air
and therefore represent intellect, judgment, rationality, and activity.
The swords, in contrast to the cups, represent the principle of action
and energy. The Ace of Swords therefore indicates the "cutting edge"
of reason. It may augur a change in your attitude or the discovery of a
new intellectual perspective on life. Finally, the pentacles are analogous
to the element of earth and therefore correspond closely to matter in
general and concerns relating to the material world. Pentacles can also
represent money and one's relationship to money. The Ace of Pentacles might represent a change in your material circumstances such as a
new employment opportunity, a change in your financial situation, or a
new perspective about your material possessions.

The major arcana evolved from the game known as Trumps
or Triumphs. This game included cards adorned with detailed designs and imagery as they are in today's tarot. The major arcana com-
prises twenty-two cards, which are numbered beginning with zero.
The exact position of each card in the major arcana has not been consistent over the years. For example, in the Rider-Waite deck the cards
of Justice and Strength are transposed in their positions as compared
with some earlier decks. In Rider-Waite's deck, Strength takes position eight, and Justice takes position eleven. In the older Marseilles
deck, however, Justice is in position eight and Strength is in position
eleven. There are various explanations for different placements of the
cards, and many debates have been sparked over the years because of
these disagreements. The most common convention today uses
Waite's positioning of cards, with the exception of his placement of the
Fool. In Waite's strategy, the Fool is placed between Judgement and
the World (cards twenty and twenty-one respectively), although most
readers today place the Fool, card zero, as the first card in the deck.
This arrangement intuitively makes sense; the Fool is the only unnum-
bered card and therefore it should precede all the numbered cards.

The fact that the tarot evolved from two different types of card games allows for the possibility of using the subsets of the entire deck in different ways for different types of readings. Although there are only two subsets of cards in the tarot, the major and the minor arcana, there are really three distinct groups of cards with which we can work in our readings: the numbered pips, the court cards, and the major arcana.

Often the major arcana cards are separated from the rest of the deck and used for readings without the minor arcana because of their unique nature and the depths of symbolism they contain. The major arcana cards can be used in readings in which there may be a desire to interact with very clear archetypal images whose meanings are more direct and powerful than those of the minor arcana. You may have a question or issue that you feel relates deeply to your innermost spiritual health and want to seek guidance from the collective unconscious by using concrete and accessible expressions of the archetypes. Or, if you are just beginning to work with the tarot, you may want to work only with the major arcana until you get more accustomed to interpreting the symbols.

Another powerful grouping of cards uses the major arcana and the court cards together without the pips. This combination gives you a total of thirty-eight cards to work with and may be a very good combination when your reading relates to people in your life or personality issues in general.

Although it is also possible to use only the minor arcana cards, usually the purpose of separating groups of cards from the deck for readings is to access the more specific and detailed insights available from the more richly symbolic images of the major arcana and court cards. Using these subsets of the tarot deck can yield powerful and specific readings that help bring light to whatever question or issue you have presented to the tarot. The version of CyberTarot included with this book contains only the major arcana cards.

THE BEST QUESTIONS

*Developing a Natural, Effective Way
to Question the Tarot*

When most people approach the tarot or consult a reader for the first time, they ask a specific question aimed at obtaining information about a choice or issue they are currently faced with. Frequently the intention is to seek advice on the best solution to their dilemma, and often this desire for specific answers is motivated by fear of making the wrong choices or by the (perhaps unconscious) desire to avoid directly facing the difficulty and taking responsibility for the decisions made. For example, a common question from people involved in relationships is "Will I marry this person?" Frequently asked questions about finances include "Will I make a lot of money?" or "Will I get a promotion?" Though there is nothing wrong with asking such specific questions of the tarot, it is important to remember that while the tarot can serve as a guide, counselor, or adviser, the final outcome of a specific situation always rests with you.

Instead of looking to the tarot to predict future events in our lives, we should concentrate on using the images as a catalyst for self-exploration and the development of a deeper knowledge of ourselves. While it is certainly possible that the tarot may in fact be able to shed light on the trends that are likely to influence us or on future events, caution must always be used when considering predictions of this kind. We can easily mislead ourselves either by fear or wishful thinking into self-fulfilling prophecies; if we become so attached to a particular prediction that all our actions eventually lead to the fulfillment of the prophecy, we lose the ability to control the direction of our own lives. This becomes dangerous because it implies the willful relinquishment of our personal freedom, and thereby our decision-making responsibility.

The ancient Greek oracle at Delphi had the phrase "Know thyself" inscribed in the stone over the portal. This admonition serves us very well indeed when working with the tarot. If we know ourselves deeply and intimately, we are not likely to be blinded by wishful thinking, led astray by false hopes, or hindered by our fears. Our freedom to make the correct decisions for our own future will be enhanced rather than diminished by using the tarot, and we will be able to control our own destiny with knowledge and the full acceptance of personal responsibility for whatever befalls us.

To avoid the dangers inherent in knowing the future (or believing we know the future), we should bring questions designed to open our inner selves to the light of our own consciousness, instead of approaching the tarot for answers to specific questions about the future or for predictions of certain outcomes. Of course, an individual must ask the right questions in order to obtain significant answers. Certain questions contain within them the implication of an answer. "How long ago did you stop beating up your brother?" directly implies that you had been consistently beating up your brother for some time. It may be a difficult question to answer; you might respond, "I didn't!" or "I never did!" which could mean either that you never beat him, or that you never stopped! If you ask, "Will John ask me to marry him?" you imply that you either want to marry him or you don't, but the answer to whether he will ask you lies outside of yourself and is completely beyond your control. If you are given an affirmative answer, you may begin to behave differently around him, and your different behavior may have the effect of either fulfilling your desire for the outcome, or of causing the very opposite to occur! So, if you really want John to ask you to marry him and your question is answered with a yes, you may begin to act in such a way that visibly demonstrates your attachment to him. You may begin to speak more openly about marriage or you may begin to hint indirectly at the subject. Of course, since the object of your desire may have a completely different agenda regarding your relationship, he may respond the way you want him to, or he may become more distant from you because of your increased attachment to him!

A better question to ask in this situation might be something like, "What do I really want from this relationship?" This question implies that the important consideration is to determine what *you* desire for the future of the relationship so you can act accordingly. In this way you are direct about seeking information from your unconscious, using the tarot as a tool to reveal your own deepest desires and to uncover any hidden concerns you may have about the relationship. The tarot, as a vehicle of communication with your personal subconscious and a bridge to the wisdom of the collective unconscious, will offer information that will help you see your situation more clearly. You may learn from your reading that you really have a strong desire to marry a particular person, but that you also have a number of concerns about your long-term compatibility, or that you are concerned about the opinions of friends or family members.

When we become clear in the knowledge of our own needs, desires, and intentions we are more readily able to direct our actions wisely or to react to unforeseen future events with clarity and calmness. The most profitable way to attain this kind of self-knowledge through the tarot is to become fluent in the language of its symbols, and to learn to ask the right questions.

Questions addressed to the tarot typically fall into a few common categories. These include love and relationships, career and finances, the family, and health and longevity. The questions that fall into these broad categories can cover a multitude of specific issues, so it is always up to you to determine the nature of the answers you are seeking from the tarot and to frame your questions appropriately, based on your current situation. You may also have questions that do not fall into any of the above categories. Again, you need to examine your inner self carefully and decide on the correct approach you should take in your reading of the tarot at any specific time. Here are a few suggestions for questions to consider when seeking wisdom from the tarot.

For love and relationship issues:

- What is my deepest desire for the outcome of this relationship?

- Is my involvement with my partner based on personal strength and love or am I in this relationship because of neediness or attachment?

- What can I do to make this relationship a more positive experience for both of us?

For career and financial concerns:

- What is my deepest desire for the type of career I wish to pursue? What kind of work would bring me the most personal satisfaction?

THE
BEST
QUESTIONS

- Are my personal power and creativity strong enough for me to make a career transition successfully or seek a new position?

- If I am unhappy with my current career or financial situation, what can I do now to improve my future prospects? How can I improve my attitude in the meantime to focus on the positive aspects of my situation?

For family issues:

- If I am having difficulties with my children, is there any way I can approach the situation differently to build more trust and reopen the channels of communication?

- If I am having problems in my relationship with my parents, is there any way I can try to help them understand me more clearly? Do I need to find a new way of communicating with my parents? Do I need to try to understand them more clearly?

- Do I have any blind spots in my perceptions of the needs of the other members of my family? How can I be more honest with myself to examine areas where I might need to make changes?

For health and longevity issues:

- Am I taking care of myself as well as I should in order to live most happily?

- Do I have any self-defeating behavior patterns that might cause me physical or psychological health problems? What can I do to develop more positive behaviors so I can be more healthy?

- Am I too influenced by external events in my life so that my stress level is higher than it should be?

Remember that these are only suggestions for general ways to query the tarot and that the specific questions suggested may not be appropriate for every individual in every situation. The important thing to keep in mind is that your interaction with the tarot is a personal matter. You will have to decide how to most effectively consult the oracle to meet your needs at the time. It is also crucial to remember to focus on using the tarot for gaining self-knowledge rather than for peering into the future. Self-knowledge is a powerful and effective tool for controlling one's own destiny and for making good decisions for the future. Knowledge of the future itself may, however, be dangerous because of our tendency to try to bring about predictions. If your concern is to try to read the future, focus on the reading you receive from the tarot as an indicator of tendencies or potentials rather than as the certain and immutable outcome of the issue you have brought to the cards. This way, you will more likely be able to observe your behavior and watch for tendencies on your part that may sway you toward fulfilling predictions. You can use the tarot as an aid to help you increase your ability to act in freedom, or you can allow the tarot to hinder your exercise of freedom. As always, the choice is yours.

Your Relationship to the Tarot Images

After you have worked with the tarot for a period of time you will begin to develop your own personal relationship with the symbols and images of the cards. This relationship will be based on an intuitive understanding of the imagery that will come from having developed a certain fluency in the language of tarot symbolism. In time you will develop the ability to get an overall sense of any reading by glancing at the combinations of cards in a spread. As you delve deeper into exploration of the individual cards and their relationship to each other and their positions in a particular spread, you will find a wealth of wisdom about yourself. Of course, as in any other kind of relationship, your relationship to the tarot will take energy and care to develop. You will need to devote a good deal of time to studying the images and learning about their symbolism to acquire enough fluency with their meanings to be able to quickly grasp the overall message of a complete tarot spread.

It will also take time to learn how to ask meaningful and appropriate questions. Don't get discouraged if it seems that you are initially not able to get much from the images. Work with the cards, study the symbols, research the meanings offered in other books on the tarot and in books about mythology, psychology, and symbolism in general. The more familiar you become with the universal language of symbols and the archetypes, the more readily you will be able to grow personally and spiritually through the use of the tarot.

A particularly useful method of gaining fluency in the language of tarot is to use the images as aids to meditation. Select a particular card for a daily meditation exercise. Gaze at the card for a while to familiarize yourself with it without thinking about its meaning. Look carefully for all the words or symbolic elements that are displayed on the card. Sometimes these symbols are obscure and hidden, like the salamanders decorating the robe of the King of Wands or the bunches of grapes adorning the outfit of the King of Pentacles. Other symbols are rather obvious, like the enormous image of the sun in the Sun card or the skeleton rider in the Death card. Try to feel the meaning of the card before you start thinking specifically about rational explanations of the symbolic elements. Does the card make you feel positive or negative? Peaceful or uneasy? Strong or weak? Fearful or courageous? Try to vocalize or write down your initial impressions of the card. If a card makes you feel unhappy, ask yourself what it is about the imagery that gives you this uncomfortable feeling. Is it the appearance of a specific image on the card? Is it the choice of colors? Why does the over-all feeling strike you in this way? Then, begin to consider the individ-ual symbols on the card. You may want to have a symbol dictionary (see the Bibliography for some examples) at hand to help you perform a more detailed translation.

Finally, read over the suggested interpretations given in this book. See if your impressions of the card agree or disagree with the in-terpretations given here. Read and study other books on the tarot as well; there is much to be gained from studying other people's analy-ses. While some insist that the explanations of the cards are clear-cut and have very specific meanings, it is in fact much more important for you to come to your own conclusions. You should study as many ap-proaches to the tarot as you feel are necessary to help you gain a deep and personal understanding of their archetypal symbolism. This way you will develop an appreciation of the cards that is based on a deep exploration of your own mind and your own reactions to the rich tarot imagery.

Think about your daily card image throughout the course of the day. Try to visualize it in your mind's eye. As your familiarity with individual cards increases, your ability to read and comprehend the messages of complete spreads will increase as well. If you become inti-mate enough with the patterns that you can imagine them in all their detail even when you are not working with them directly, you will have developed a mastery of those language elements that make up the basic structure of tarot readings. Then, when you work with groups of cards arranged in spreads, you will be able to make endless associa-tions among the images of the cards before you. Previously unnoticed patterns will suddenly become very clear to you, and you will see con-nections that will open up new ways of perceiving your life. You will begin to notice relationships among things in the world apart from the tarot that you may not have noticed before. Working with the tarot in this way will allow you to develop an entirely new way of viewing the world based on the recognition of the archetypes and symbols present everywhere in our lives. You will begin to recognize the allegorical possibilities in the simplest things and events of daily life.

When you are able to translate full spreads intuitively and instinctively you will have gained a command of the language of tarot that will give you a key to comprehending many hidden truths about yourself. As you grow in self-awareness and confidence, you will eventually learn to work with others in helping them understand their own psychological inclinations. Through your ability to utilize the medium of the tarot to access the archetypes present in the collective unconscious, you can bring light and clarity not only to yourself but to others as well.

THE THUMBNAIL HISTORY OF TAROT

*T*he origins of the tarot cards are buried deep in the mists of an obscure and fantastic history. Popular legends about the tarot associate the symbols of the cards with ancient Egypt, citing apparent similarities between the tarot images and the rich symbolic characters of the hieroglyphic language, the brilliant carvings of great ancient temples, and the colorful wall paintings of the tombs of the pharaohs. Other speculation links the tarot with the symbolic systems of India or other countries of the Far East, and suggests that the cards were brought to Europe in the Middle Ages by bands of Gypsies who used them for fortune-telling. Still other conjectures draw links between the tarot and the classical Jewish mystical tradition of the cabala. Despite the appeal and fascination of these theories of the origin of tarot, the known history of the cards may be far more mundane than these imaginative musings lead us to believe. However, despite the efforts of historians and scholars to diffuse the creative speculations of tarot enthusiasts, the legends surrounding the tarot continue to remain influential. Opinions regarding the origins of the tarot symbols and the connections between the tarot and the philosophical systems of exotic or extinct cultures continue to captivate an astonished audience.

The first known historical references to the use of playing cards date from the end of the Middle Ages. The earliest comments about games played with cards were recorded in sermons given by monks who condemned card games (as well as other games of "chance" such as dice) as being detrimental to the spiritual life of good Christians. However, despite many pious attempts to squelch their popularity, the games caught on and by the middle of the sixteenth century card games were widely played throughout Europe. During the period from the sixteenth through the late seventeenth centuries, variations of the games Trumps, Tarocco, and Tarot were played throughout Europe with decks of approximately twenty-two cards, particularly in the courts of kings and nobles, who were able to commission colorful, gilded decks for their amusement. Other card games with less colorful imagery and approximately fifty-six cards were being circulated as well and were played more widely by the common people because of their simplicity of design, availability, and lower cost. At some point, the two decks were combined, forming the basis of what we now know as the seventy-eight-card tarot deck.

Although many have speculated about the early use of the tarot for divination, most historical evidence indicates that tarot was used in its first centuries primarily for entertainment. However, there were considerations about the possible uses of the trump cards for moral instruction by monks who, in earlier centuries, had condemned the use of card games outright. In addition, there are indications that players of the game of Trumps may have used the cards in parlor games designed to explore and understand the personalities of the participants. These players would select cards to represent each other and then explore together the reasons for their choices. So, although the widespread use of tarot for divination and self-knowledge seems to have been absent in the earliest years of its known history, nonetheless the symbols were occasionally perceived to have meaning beyond simple amusement and may have been used for informal "personality studies" and self-exploration.

Despite the tremendous popularity of Tarot, Tarocco, and Trumps during the fifteenth, sixteenth, and seventeenth centuries, by the early eighteenth century these games had all but disappeared into oblivion. The cards remained in relative obscurity until the end of the eighteenth century, when a Frenchman named Antoine Court de Gebelin rediscovered the tarot and revived interest in the cards. His rediscovery produced a resurgence of interest in the game, but from a different perspective than that which influenced the earlier fanciers of the cards.

Court de Gebelin interpreted the card images as remnants of an ancient Egyptian symbolic system that had been forgotten over the ages but that remained hidden in the images of the tarot. Despite the fact that the Egyptian hieroglyphic language had not yet been deciphered and the meaning of the ancient texts was nothing more than speculation, Court de Gebelin proposed that the tarot symbols were derived from Egyptian culture and served as a secret record of the wisdom of the ancients. In fact, images such as the sun played a central role in the religion of the ancient Egyptians, and many of the great surviving temples and documents depict images of the sun god Ra traversing the sky in his great celestial chariot.

Although Court de Gebelin had no actual historical basis for his theory of the tarot's origin, nevertheless it is possible to see how such a connection could be made. His explanation of the strange symbols of the tarot thus began the legend of their ancient Egyptian origin. He also laid the foundation for further exploration of the philosophical, psychological, and magical uses of the cards, and inspired further speculation (often with no other basis than the whim of the theorist, or the popular conceptions of the time) into the history of the tarot.

Following Court de Gebelin's initial correlation between ancient Egypt and the tarot, other intellectuals and self-styled historians of the tarot elaborated on the claims of the ancient origins of the cards. Throughout the Romantic period of the nineteenth century, the tarot became the subject of numerous unlikely speculations involving its connections not only with Egypt, but also with the Far East, India, the Hermetica of the early Christian era, gnosticism, the practice of alchemy, and even the mythical lost civilization of Atlantis. The most important element of all these theories of the tarot's origin is the fact that during this period the powerful, archetypal symbolism of the tarot images became more widely recognized and the tarot was no longer viewed as simply a game but rather as a key to understanding the deeper truths of the human experience.

The consideration of the tarot as a practical tool for developing knowledge of oneself was furthered greatly by the work of Eliphas Levi during the mid-nineteenth century. Levi's elaboration of the philosophical connections between the tarot and the mystical tradition of the cabala furthered the esoteric understanding of the tarot images. Although the cabala historically has little or nothing to do with the tarot, cabalistic philosophy and imagery were easily worked into Levi's interpretations of the tarot. One of the most obvious correlations was that the major arcana consisted of twenty-two cards, the same as the number of letters in the Hebrew alphabet. This similarity, although very superficial at first glance, was offered as a primary element of a hypothesis that the tarot was in fact a remnant of the wisdom of the ancient priesthood of Israel.

The story postulates that the priests recorded their hidden knowledge on strips of parchment or leather around the time that the Temple of Jerusalem was destroyed. These parchment records were eventually transferred to cards, which were carried from the Middle East into Europe by Gypsies in medieval times. Many scholars of both subjects tend to dismiss these allegations of a tarot-cabala connection. However, the philosophical interpretations linking the two esoteric schools of thought have been painstakingly developed and are very influential among students of the tarot. Whether or not there are actual historical relationships between the cabala and the tarot, the integration of the metaphysical knowledge of these diverse systems has provided much in the way of interesting and creative philosophy.

The development of the tarot as a tool for psychological understanding was furthered at the end of the nineteenth century by a group called the Hermetic Order of the Golden Dawn. The Golden Dawn was founded as a secret society dedicated to the quest for mystical and metaphysical knowledge. The Order created and practiced unusual magical rituals derived from many of the mystical traditions of the world, and its members (among whom was the famous poet W. B. Yeats) displayed tremendous creativity in the area of metaphysical philosophy. Despite the fact that the Order of the Golden Dawn was rife with internal dissension from its earliest days, it remains one of the greatest influences on the subsequent history and development of the tarot. One of the more illustrious members of this society, Arthur Edward Waite, is the creative force behind the development of the Rider-Waite tarot deck, which is used in CyberTarot.

In 1903 A. E. Waite assumed leadership of the London temple of the Golden Dawn and shifted the focus of the society from a preoccupation with magic to an orientation based on mysticism and alchemy. The magnum opus in alchemical traditions is primarily concerned with enlightening the soul and mind, rather than controlling external circumstances through magic. The image of transforming lead into gold is actually an allegory for the transformation of the human soul. This transformation necessitates a shift away from the psychological attachment to the material world, toward the realization and experience of the essential unity of all things in the universe. This change in the character of the order resulted in a schism in which a number of prominent members (including Yeats) left the Golden Dawn to form their own magical societies.

Despite the rift in the Golden Dawn, Waite pressed on with his new agenda and in 1910 released his book, *The Pictorial Key to the Tarot,* along with his revised tarot deck with drawings by Pamela Colman Smith. A primary consideration in the design of Waite's book and deck is the integration of various mystical, metaphysical, and philosophical systems into the imagery used in the cards. Waite himself was a meticulous scholar who not only attempted to use his tarot as a repository for the secret knowledge of the Order of the Golden Dawn but also made a concerted effort to correct the written history of the tarot and debunk the myths that had surrounded it. Much of the symbolism in the Rider-Waite tarot deck is based on the tradition of alchemy, and the true purpose of the tarot in Waite's eyes was always that of lifting the consciousness to higher planes of knowledge than could be reached through ordinary means of study. Waite was adamant in his attempts to dissociate the tarot from fortune-telling and charlatanism. Waite says in *The Pictorial Key to the Tarot,* "The true Tarot is symbolism; it speaks no other language and offers no other signs."

Waite distinguished himself from many contemporary commentators by attempting to separate myth and legend from the known history of the tarot. Instead of casually accepting, for example, the Egyptian theory of Court de Gebelin or the cabalistic hypothesis encouraged by Eliphas Levi some fifty years earlier, Waite acknowledged that the history of tarot could not be traced further back than the fourteenth century. His tarot deck has become the single most popular and influential deck in print and continues to inspire newer designs by virtue of its depth of symbolism and simplicity of design.

Another important characteristic of the Rider-Waite deck is

the fact that it is one of the first decks to depict complete images on the fifty-six cards of the minor arcana. In earlier decks, particularly the widely used Marseilles deck, the minor arcana cards were decorated in very simple designs, much more like modern playing cards. For example, in the Marseilles deck, a card such as the Four of Cups depicts the simple image of a group of four cups arranged in an ordered pattern. In the Rider-Waite deck, the Four of Cups portrays a young man in the midst of a deep state of concentration who is apparently faced with a difficult decision. The use of complete, detailed images for the minor arcana, though somewhat novel at the time of Waite's publication, provides the reader with a great depth of symbolism and imagery. Later tarot designers have followed Waite's example, and most decks produced in the twentieth century use complete images for the minor arcana.

Although the works of A. E. Waite and subsequent scholars have, for all practical purposes, refuted the mythological histories of the tarot, nevertheless the romantic notions of the tarot's ancient origins persist and remain quite popular to this day. Despite the fact that the tarot deck as we know it was probably not designed and transported to Western society from the ancient East, the idea that the images represent an ancient fount of human knowledge may in itself be more important than the proof of that concept as historical fact.

The tenacity of legendary explanations for the origins of the tarot speaks directly to the human need for mystery and symbolic expression. And the images of the tarot themselves are, without question, a representative sample of the archetypes that shape and define the human experience. An archetype is, as we have discussed, a concept that pervades the consciousness of all humanity because it represents something common to universal human experience.

In the tarot, we see archetypes such as Death (an inescapable and often frightening fact of the human condition), the Devil (an anthropomorphism of the reality of evil), and the Empress (a mother fig-

ure in the strongest sense). It is these archetypes that so strongly connect the consciousness of humanity with that of our ancient ancestors,
and it is these archetypes that keep us close to the ancients despite our
contemporary fascination with technology, and our belief in ourselves
as somehow different or more advanced than our predecessors. And,
of course, it is these archetypes that form the basis of speculations
linking the tarot with the wisdom and knowledge of our ancient
forebears.

In a sense, then, the tarot does in fact have its origins in the
mysterious history of lost civilizations. Ancient peoples struggled to
understand themselves and their world just as contemporary peoples
search for the same knowledge. Symbols, art, literature, and other expressions of the imagination are attempts to grasp the significance and
the meaning of the archetypes that move our souls as we journey
through the mystery of life. The tarot is but another means of estab-
lishing a meaningful relationship with the archetypes that shape our
destinies, another tool for expressing their importance to the universal
experience of mankind.

UNDERSTANDING THE SYMBOLS OF THE MAJOR AND MINOR ARCANA

*I*n this section, suggested interpretations are offered for the seventy-eight cards in the complete Rider-Waite tarot deck. These interpretations are starting points for your own exploration of the meanings of the tarot. Do not allow yourself to be limited by what is offered here; instead, let these suggested interpretations open the door of your imagination and intuition so you can find what is meaningful for you in each card. Study the images, learn their obvious symbolism as well as their hidden secrets. The interpretations given here can be a diving board into the great wellspring of the archetypes that live deep within your own consciousness.

THE MAJOR ARCANA

The Fool

Words: *Bright sun, golden sky, white rose, white dog, white mountain peaks, cliffs, wooden staff, leather knapsack, bird embroidered on satchel, flowers on Fool's garment.*

Phrases: *The Fool is the first card in the tarot deck and as such represents new beginnings. Symbolically, the Fool begins the journey of self-exploration upon which we embark when we come to the tarot for knowledge about ourselves. The card pictures a young man about to step off the edge of a cliff. He displays a carefree attitude, which is demonstrated in his willingness to take such risks without regard to the consequences. The Fool is an innocent (as we all are at the beginning of life's journey) and because of his innocence may be somewhat naive. He carries a small satchel, which contains the few possessions he owns, and the white rose in his left hand represents purity of heart. Despite his naïveté, the Fool is blessed with the protection of divine grace, symbolized by the sun shining on his back. There is a sense about him that even if he were to fall off the cliff, he would not be injured because he is a holy child of God, cared for and protected by the power of the divine. This card is reminiscent of the figure of St. Francis of Assisi, who in his simplicity, poverty, and purity of heart called himself "God's Fool." What do you see of yourself in him? What aspects of his character might you want to adopt in yourself?*

The Magician

Words: *White cloak, red robe, white lilies, red roses, flowered canopy, red table, pentacle, cup, sword, wand, ouroboros as magician's belt, lemniscate, magic wand upraised in his right hand, left hand pointing down toward earth, golden sky.*

Phrases: *The Magician is the second card in the deck, and is the first numbered card. He is the bridge between the world of the spirit and the world of humanity. His right hand holds a staff upraised toward the sky and his left hand points to the earth. He is the transmitter of spiritual power, the mediator between God and mankind. Over his head is the symbol of eternity (lemniscate), and around his waist is a snake biting its own tail (ouroboros), another symbol of eternity. His magical table holds all four suits of the tarot, each of which represents one of the four primordial elements of the alchemists: earth, air, fire, and water. His robe is white, symbolizing the purity and innocence found in the Fool, but his cloak is red, representing worldly experience and knowledge. In the bed of flowers at his feet this duality is repeated in the mix of pure white lilies and thorny red roses. The magician represents the bridge between the opposites; he is a composite of innocence and experience, spirit and matter, heaven and earth. He is experienced, unlike the Fool, and is a teacher of hidden truths. When you encounter the Magician along life's journey, you have encountered a wise sage who can help you find your way. Perhaps he indicates a need to find a balance between the material and the spiritual aspects of your nature. Or he might be an encouraging sign of the strength you need at a difficult time. What do you see in the power of the Magician?*

The High Priestess

Words: Blue sky, black column, white column, cross, crown depicting stages of the moon, golden crescent moon, blue and white robes, veil hung from the columns, pomegranates, palm leaves, scroll with "TORA" written on it.

Phrases: The High Priestess is the union of opposites. Unlike the Magician, who bridges the gap between heaven and earth, the High Priestess contains this duality within herself. Thus she is flanked by two columns, one white and one black. She is the inner spiritual guide who lives within each of us. Behind her is a veil covered with pomegranates, a fruit of many seeds that represents fertility and plenty and is the symbol of the Greek goddess Persephone. At her feet is a crescent moon, and this feature, along with the white robe and blue cloak, reminds us of Mary, mother of Jesus, the woman of paradox who is both virgin and mother. She wears a cross on her chest and holds a copy of the Torah, the body of wisdom and law in the Jewish scripture. These remind us of the spiritual power she possesses. The High Priestess represents our unconscious, the teacher who reveals truth to us only in glimpses and in our dreams. She does not flaunt or exhibit her power openly as does the Magician, but rather represents the quiet, often misunderstood spiritual power within each of us. When you see her, ask yourself, "Is there something I am overlooking? Is there something within me desiring expression that I have not listened to?" The High Priestess indicates the need to look deep within ourselves for guidance and the answers to our questions.

The Empress

Words: Twelve-star crown, royal scepter, wheat or corn fields, trees, river flowing through forest, red couch, heart-shaped pillow or shield, symbol of Venus at her feet, white robe, pomegranates.

Phrases: The Empress is the arche-typal earth mother, the anima, the feminine principle. She is full figured, possibly pregnant, and is surrounded by lush greenery and fields of ripe wheat or corn. Below her couch is a heart-shaped pillow or shield with the symbol of Venus emblazoned upon it, and her flowing robe is decorated with pomegranates, a symbol of fertility. In the forest behind her a river flows freely with water, the

symbol of life. Her upraised hand holds a scepter, which demonstrates her power and authority over the things of this earth. Whereas the High Priest-ess represents the unconscious and the spirit, the Empress represents the earth and all the bounty and fruitfulness thereof. Her meaning suggests richness and fulfillment, the satisfaction of physical needs and desires. As with any card, there is the potential for excess in her abundance, and when you see her you must ask yourself how her rich, sumptuous imagery speaks to your heart. Are you perhaps too immersed in the material world? Or does she promise you a fulfillment that you have been seeking but have not yet discovered? What does she tell you about yourself? Material and spiritual interests must be balanced in order to experience a fulfilled life, and neither should be taken to the extreme.

The Emperor

Words: Red sky, barren mountains, orb, scepter, red robe, jeweled crown, ram's heads at four corners of throne.

THE EMPEROR.

Phrases: The Emperor is the complement to the Empress. He is the masculine principle, the animus, the patriarch. He represents power and authority, and his stern attitude is quite a departure from the sensual beauty of the Empress. Behind his throne are barren mountains, a symbol of the lofty heights of which he is master. The throne itself is decorated with four rams' heads, representing intellectual heights and sure-footedness in climbing the lofty crags. His right hand holds an ankh, Egyptian symbol of life, and in his left is an orb representing the world over which he rules. In his extreme form the Emperor can be cold and unfeeling, relying solely on his laws and pronouncements for judgment. In this sense he is inflexible and stern, yet his age indicates an understanding and ability to express compassion gleaned from many years of experience and rulership. What do you see in his powerful persona? Is there something in you that is inflexible and judgmental, or is his power indicative of achievement and success despite many hardships?

The Hierophant

Words: Golden tiara (three-tiered crown), red robe, white garment, three crosses on vestments, keys of St. Peter at his feet, two columns, scepter, right hand upraised in gesture of blessing, two priests, garments decorated with lilies and roses.

Phrases: The Hierophant is similar to the Magician in that he represents a link between ourselves and the divine. The role of the Hierophant is traditionally that of the mediator between God and mankind, the high priest on earth. As such he represents the spiritual teacher who helps us come into contact with the divine. Unlike the Magician, who simply points the way, the Hierophant is a trusted guide, one who will take us by the hand and lead us to our spiritual goal. He also represents tradition, the orthodox, organized methods of nurturing spirituality. Regardless of your religious background, the Hierophant represents the spirituality you were taught from childhood, the religious traditions that are your heritage. The darker side of this card can represent authoritarian control and domination of religious expression. If you encounter the Hierophant, you may need to examine your spiritual life, particularly in terms of the communal expression of that spirituality. Perhaps there is a need to return to our spiritual roots and explore forgotten traditions. Or there may be the opposite need: to learn to stand on your own spiritual feet, as it were, and explore the spiritual depths of your own psyche apart from any communal expression of faith. What feelings does the Hierophant elicit when you see him? What is he trying to tell you?

The Lovers

Words: Golden sun, blue sky, angel, fruit tree with snake coiled around trunk, tree with branches of fire, mountain, green earth.

Phrases: The lovers represent relationships in our lives, particularly intimate and/or sexual relationships. This card indicates situations in our lives where love is primarily important and may reflect the state of our relationships at the time. The lovers are blessed and protected by the angel in the clouds above them, and the sun shines brightly overhead, bringing warmth and security. The earth at their feet is green and fertile and suggests life and happiness. However, as with all the cards, there are negative aspects to be considered in the symbolism of the lovers. The snake in the fruit tree behind the woman suggests the story of Adam and Eve, the fall of humanity from grace, and the temptations of the world. The Hindu concept of maya, which refers to the illusory nature of the material world, is suggested in the temptation of the fruit. Behind the man, on the other hand, is a black tree with flames for leaves. The flames represent the fires of passion that burn within each of us and that can cause spiritual imbalance in our lives if we allow them free reign over us. The world is both a blessing and a curse, and it contains the potentiality for both good and evil. The lovers represent both the beauty and the corruption of our physical, bodily aspect. How do the images speak to you? What is their relationship to the other cards in your reading? Do they indicate a need for more balance in your life? Or do they suggest worldly fulfillment and happiness?

71

The Chariot

Words: Black and white sphinxes, golden star in crown, moon-shaped epaulets containing faces; city in background, golden sky, blue canopy with stars, winged moon at top of a shield on front of a chariot.

Phrases: The charioteer in this card is a young man whose face bears the unmistakable countenance of determination, focus, and ambition. He is related to the Fool in that he is anxious for new experiences and for adventure, yet he differs from the Fool because he is focused and has a clear goal in mind. He represents youthful passion, potency, the desire to succeed and accomplish great goals, without the naïveté of the Fool. His canopy is covered with stars and his uniform suggests celestial power and spiritual assistance because of the crescent moons on his epaulets and the stars in his crown. The Chariot indicates not only the pursuit but the nearly assured success of the driver's ambition through the exercise of a focused and determined will. The duality of this ambition is represented by the sphinxes at the front of the vehicle. The black sphinx is the negative aspect of an overambitious desire to reach a goal at any cost. The white sphinx is the positive aspect of this same desire. Does the Chariot indicate a need to embrace a goal and pursue it with vigor? Or does he suggest that perhaps your determination is excessive and possibly detrimental to the health of other aspects of your life? How does this image reflect your inner and outer circumstances?

Strength

Words: *Golden sky, red lion, blue mountain, lemniscate, white robe, garlands of flowers, trees and greenery in background.*

Phrases: *This card represents strength, determination, and power in a manner similar to the Chariot. However, the differences are obvious at a glance. Instead of a powerful, focused warrior we encounter a gentle woman, unarmed and without the protection of armor. She overcomes the lion with a quiet strength that can come only from within. Where the Chariot represents outer strength and will, the card of Strength represents inner power, the power of the human spirit to overcome any obstacle. That the woman represents the spirit is manifest by her white robe, depicting purity, and the symbol of eternity above her head. She wears a belt and crown of flowers and stands unprotected in an open green field. The Chariot indicates that worldly success is possible if our goals are pursued with focus and energy. The Strength card tells us that our deeper power comes from within. The lion represents inner and/or outer challenges that attempt to hinder us in our life's journey. This card tells us that we can overcome any difficulty if we utilize the inner strength of our spirit and trust in the divine power of the universe for our energy and sustenance. When this card is encountered in a reading, it may be an indication of the need to deepen our spiritual life. Or it may be a reminder to those of us who have lost sight of our inner strength.*

The Hermit

Words: *Blue-green sky, gray color-less robe, golden staff, lantern, hexa-gram, white mountain crags.*

Phrases: *The Hermit is the wise spirit within. He, like the Fool, stands at the edge of a precipice on the peak of a barren mountain. But unlike the inno-cent, naive Fool who carelessly steps over the edge, the Hermit holds the staff of wisdom in one hand and a light in the other to give direction to those who do not know the way. The Hermit is the ancient spirit that lives within us through the ex-istence of the collective unconscious, the universal mind that guides us through the darkness with its clear light. The Hermit represents the deepest part of ourselves, that part which knows what to do in times of decision, knows the right way to respond to the world and its challenges. The Hermit is the seer who guides us during difficult times, the prophet who speaks the voice of conscience to us when we lose our way. When we encounter the Hermit in a reading, we should take it as an indication that the answers we seek can be found within our own hearts. How does the Wise Man speak to you as you encounter his visage?*

The Wheel of Fortune

Words: *Four symbols in corners represent four evangelists, four seasons, four directions; gray clouds, blue sky, wheel, sphinx holding a sword, red jackal-headed figure, snake, upon the wheel the word "TARO" and in Hebrew the name of God, "YHVH."*

WHEEL of FORTUNE.

Phrases: *The Wheel of Fortune, perhaps more strongly than any other card, has a dual aspect of light and dark, good and ill. This card represents the circular nature of time as reflected in the phrase "What goes around comes around." Our lives are full of ups and downs and none of these periods of difficulty or prosperity lasts forever. There will always be change in our lives; we must learn to adapt or we will be left behind as the world moves along without us. The Wheel of Fortune clearly indicates the transitory nature of the world and gives us an opportunity to reexamine our lives to determine where we are in the cycle at the time we encounter the card. If we are at the bottom we may need to prompt ourselves into moving forward and bringing about positive changes to our situation. If we are riding high at the top of the cycle, the card may be reminding us to be grateful for what we have and not be callous or take our good fortune for granted. This card is filled with symbols. The four beings in each corner are the symbols of the four gospel writers of the New Testament. The wheel itself bears both the letters "TARO" for the tarot, and the Hebrew letters of the name of God, "YHVH." The sphinx at the top of the wheel represents success and good fortune and reminds us of the sphinxes in the Chariot card. The devil at the bottom of the wheel is there to keep us alert, to help make us aware that all things are subject to change.*

Justice

Words: *Two columns, golden crown, golden sky, upraised sword, scales of justice, red robe.*

Phrases: *Justice represents harmony and balance. In all the cards, as we encounter the positive and negative aspects of life, we must choose between right and wrong, darkness and light. Justice represents the balance that we must all create in order to live healthy and fulfilled lives. The woman sits between two columns, as do the High Priestess and the Hierophant. In her right hand she holds a two-edged sword representing duality, and in her left hand are the scales used to find balance and harmony between the often conflicting elements of our lives. When you encounter the card of Justice, the meaning to be understood is not necessarily that you have a choice to make but rather that you must look at the areas of imbalance or excess in your life to determine where more moderation and equilibrium can bring peace to replace turmoil. Does your life reflect the principles embodied in the concept of Justice?*

The Hanged Man

Words: Red tights, blue cloak, legs crossed, golden halo, tree, garlands of flowers and fruits.

Phrases: The Hanged Man appears to be a captive, suffering an undeserved punishment under the power of an unknown malicious force. This initial impression generally leaves a reader with the uneasy feeling that the card portends disaster or trouble. However, when viewed more closely, the positive aspects of the card become more evident. The young man bears a peaceful countenance upon his face, much more the look of a man content with his fate than at the mercy of unknown powers. He also has a bright yellow halo around his head, suggestive of his purity and innocence. The Hanged Man is a willing victim, someone who has chosen the path of sacrifice to accomplish a higher goal. He hangs upside down upon a cross, like St. Peter, who was crucified upside down for bearing witness to the message of Jesus. The Hanged Man represents the willingness to forsake the temptations of instant gratification for a higher cause, and because of his willing sacrifice he accomplishes the goals he has in his heart. When we encounter the Hanged Man, we should consider areas in our lives where we may need to act in a more selfless manner either for the benefit of others or for the fulfillment of our own deeper needs. In contrast, we may need to examine our lives for areas in which we are giving too much to others at the expense of our own mental and spiritual well-being. What emotions does the image of the Hanged Man stir in you?

77

Death

Words: *Skeleton rider, black suit of armor, white horse, black flag, white rose, rising or setting sun, two columns, papal figure praying, dead king, crown and scepter, dying children in foreground, river with a ship appearing just under the horse's belly.*

Phrases: *The Death card is probably the most feared and misunderstood of all the cards in the tarot deck. In general, people tend to take the meaning of this card far too literally and fear that the indication is for the death of either themselves or others. Relax! The card of Death can be one of the most fruitful and positive cards in the deck. Death is a symbol of the ending of some phase or aspect of our lives that may bring about the beginning of something far more valuable and important. If we encounter this card in a reading it may be an indication that we need to learn to let go of unhealthy attachments in our lives to pave the way to a fuller, more fulfilled life of deeper meaning and significance. The Death card is a card of change, a card of transition. We are transformed by the death of old ways of thinking and by releasing ourselves from clinging attachments that restrain our further growth. The Death card represents the clearing of the old to usher in the new and therefore should be welcomed as a positive, cleansing, transformative force in our lives. "Unless the seed should fall to the ground and die, it shall never bring forth fruit" should be the guiding spirit under which this card is understood. The death and clearing away of limiting factors can open the door to a wider, more satisfying experience of life. What changes are you experiencing? What phase of your life is passing away? Will this change enable you to have a richer experience of life? Or, more actively, what can you do to bring about positive change in your life? Notice, the sun is setting in the distance. Or is it rising?*

Temperance

Words: *Blue mountains, golden crown, path leading from the water, two cups exchanging water, circle at woman's forehead, square containing a triangle upon her white robe, aura surrounding her head, green plants.*

Phrases: *Temperance, like Justice, indicates the need for balance and tranquility to achieve and experience fulfillment in our lives. The angel in the image has one foot on a stone and the other in the river. In this stance she represents the need to "test the waters" before jumping headlong into unknown circumstances. Here she tempers the whimsical flight of the Fool, who jumps without giving a second thought. In her hands are two cups, which she uses to mix water. One cup can be thought of as holding hot water and the other cold water. The temperate individual mixes the opposites and finds a balance in life by avoiding extremes. Behind her is the Royal Road of Wisdom, which, if followed in the spirit of Temperance, will lead us to the golden crown of self-knowledge and self-mastery in the distance. How does the image of Temperance speak to you? Does it indicate a need to find more balance in your life? Or does it teach you that compromise is not only necessary but healthy in your choices?*

The Devil

Words: *Inverted pentacle, rams' horns, wings of a bat, flaming torch, square block as throne, chains, woman with a tail of fruit, man with tail of fire.*

Phrases: *The card of the Devil represents those hidden forces of negativity that constrain us and deceive us into thinking we are imprisoned by external forces. The Devil is an inner force within each of us; he is an embodiment of our fears, addictions, and other harmful impulses. The people chained at his feet are entranced with the paralyzing fear of his illusory power and therefore stand still with hopelessness and a numb appearance. However, the chains hang loosely around their necks, an indication that liberation is within their grasp if they can only break free of the hypnotic attachment to the temptations offered by the Devil. The Devil is a master of deception and illusion. The chains he binds us with are not real; we have given him any power he has over us. When we encounter the Devil in a reading, we must ask ourselves where we are "stuck" in life. We often fall prey to despair and the thought that we are controlled by external forces, but we forge our own chains of imprisonment and powerlessness. What are the addictions or attachments restraining you from experiencing the freedom of the Fool? Are you giving yourself over to the illusion of helplessness and despair? You have the power within to set yourself free from the bondage of the Devil. What can you do to free yourself from his deception?*

The Tower

Words: *Golden crown, gray clouds, black sky, lightning bolt, flames from tower's windows, tongues of flame in the sky, blue garments, red cloak, mountainous cliffs.*

Phrases: *The Tower follows the card of the Devil and represents the breaking of his bonds. The Tower can be seen as a place of imprisonment and illusion, and the destruction of this edifice paves the way to an experience of freedom in our lives. In addition, the Tower can signify our ego and the illusion of considering ourselves "above" others. When the tower of deception, ego, and illusion is destroyed, we are freed to face truth and reality without the trappings of false attachments. The sudden destruction of the tower represents the immediacy of change, and the often disorienting effects of that change. However, in order to become free and empowered human beings, we must be willing to accept the trials of personal transformation and accept even radical disruptions of the status quo. The Tower is about inspiration, freedom, reality, and the release from bondage. Whereas the Devil may have indicated a need to make a change, the Tower represents the present reality of change. Are you undergoing a major shift in consciousness? Are you beginning to see things in a new way? The Tower tells us that things are being "stirred up" in our lives. The important question to ask is whether we can accept this change and move forward into a more positive psychological state, one where personal freedom is the rule.*

The Star

Words: *Blue sky, seven white stars, one large golden star, pool of water, fruit tree, golden bird, hill, green earth, mountains.*

Phrases: *The Star is a card of harmony and balance, much like the card of Temperance. However, because the Star follows the card of the Tower, it also represents the end of a period of change and turmoil. The Star is a card of fulfillment, peace of mind, mental and emotional stability. Like Temperance, the woman in the card holds two containers of water, but in this case she pours the water out to nourish the earth and continue the cycle of fertility, which is repre-*

sented by the lush greenery around her. Also like Temperance, she has one foot on land and the other in the water. The water represents the spiritual realm, and the land is a symbol of the material world. She represents the wisdom of experience and the calm certainty of self-confidence, and self-knowledge. She will not rush carelessly into the unknown like the Fool but will remain calm and in peace because of her wisdom. The Star is a guiding light within us, the deepest part of our self, which knows that we are under the protection and guidance of the divine spirit. What reaction does she call forth from you as you encounter her peaceful image?

The Moon

THE MOON.

Words: Blue night sky, golden moon with human face; drops of dew, two columns, path leading from water, green earth, blue mountains, crayfish or crab, wolf, dog.

Phrases: The Moon is the card of intuition, dreams, and the unconscious. The moon provides light as a reflection of the sun, yet this light is dim, uncertain, and only vaguely illuminates our path as we journey toward higher consciousness. Similarly, our dreams, intuitions, and inner promptings lead us forward toward higher levels of understanding if we listen carefully and use our judgment to help interpret the veiled messages of the unconscious. The water at the base of the card represents the inner ocean of the collective unconscious, from which a crab or crayfish emerges. This creature represents the often disturbing images that appear from our inner depths, just as the dog and wolf at the beginning of the path represent the tamed and the wild aspects of our minds. The path leads between two towers into the mountains in the distance. The towers represent good and evil, much like the columns flanking the High Priestess. The mountains in the distance represent the higher knowledge we seek under the illumination of the Moon. How do you respond to the promptings of the unconscious? Do you attempt to understand the vague suggestions of your dreams, or do you simply ignore these messages? How does this card affect you? What wisdom can you find by listening carefully to the images within your unconscious?

The Sun

THE SUN.

Words: Blue sky, golden sun with straight and wavy rays, sunflowers, child riding white horse, large red banner.

Phrases: The Sun is an image of optimism and fulfillment, the dawn that follows our darkest night. As the source of all life on earth, the Sun represents the blessings of divinity, the source of life itself. The child playing joyfully in the foreground represents the happiness of our inner spirit when we are in tune with our truest self. The white horse upon which the child rides represents strength and purity of spirit. The sunflowers in the background represent life and the fruitfulness of the spirit under the nourishment of the Sun. This is one of the most positive cards in the tarot deck, and should be received with joy and thankfulness if encountered in a reading. The only negative aspect about this card concerns our tendency to become attached to the "good times" when we are experiencing them and to forget the trials we survived in order to get there. In your bliss, do not forget the trials that have passed or that others may be experiencing. Compassion and understanding are the fruits of experience and should never be forgotten. How does this happy card fit in with the rest of your reading? Is it tempered or balanced by another card that portends either past, present, or future challenges?

Judgement

Words: *Angel, golden trumpet, gray clouds, white banner with red cross; red wings of the angel, deep blue sky, white mountain peaks, bodies rising, graves scattered on blue earth and in water.*

Phrases: *Judgement relates to the necessity of decision. You are faced with a choice and the time has come to deal with the questions before you; it's time to take action toward developing your greater good. The card also indicates an inner awakening, the beginnings of a new way of living and experiencing the world. Something that was lying dormant within us, some unconscious knowledge or truth is finally being awakened and brought into the light. The Judgement card has positive and negative aspects. In the positive sense we are being awakened from a long sleep, a period during which we lacked clarity, and now insight is dawning upon us in a psychic rebirth and resurrection. In the negative sense, we are being called to account for past actions and to justify in the light of truth what we have done in the past. Judgement speaks of a time of reckoning, a time of bringing to light those things which were hidden. The psychological process of self-revelation often brings relief and joy, yet it is frequently a difficult process in which we encounter darker aspects of our personality, which were hidden out of fear or self-defense. What are the choices and challenges you must face as you encounter the card of Judgement? Most importantly, what is your judgment of yourself, your own self-appraisal?*

The World

Words: *Four symbols in corners represent four evangelists, four seasons, four directions; gray clouds, bright blue sky, green oval-shaped wreath, red ribbons, woman within the wreath, two white magical wands, hair embroidered with flowers.*

Phrases: *The card of the World signifies fulfillment, the end of the journey, the final completion of the cycle of time. We have arrived and have accomplished our purpose. The Fool's journey is completed in the World; his wisdom and experience is now complete. The four beings, representing the gospel writers of the New Testament, appear again in the corners of this card and their presence here reminds us of the Wheel of Fortune. The World card is very much associated with the Wheel, the cyclical progression of time, and our human experience. The dancing figure in the center of the wreath wears a purple robe signifying royalty and bliss. She rejoices with us in the completion of the journey and celebrates not only this completion but also the new beginnings it promises. The World is a card of self-knowledge, of joyous wisdom, and of freedom from the bondage of false attachments. The circle represents the culmination of a long journey, the enlightenment experienced by the seeker who has struggled for the truth. Yet the circle also represents the ever-turning Wheel of Life and we must remember even in our most satisfied, fulfilled times (as well as in our most difficult times) that the cycle will continue. Change will come again, and the Fool's journey will be started once more. Where are you in your journey as you encounter this card?*

THE MINOR ARCANA

*T*he minor arcana cards form a subset of the tarot deck that evolved from a separate deck than that of the major arcana. Because the decks were initially separate, it is possible to do complete tarot readings using either subset of the deck, although the major arcana cards are usually preferred for such readings because they have traditionally contained the most complete collections of symbols.

Ace of Wands

Words: *Gray sky, red wand budding with leaves, luminous white hand, dark gray clouds, rich green earth, red barren hills, castle on a hill, small trees, winding river.*

Phrases: *The suit of wands corresponds to the alchemical element of fire. Fire is a force of consuming power that has the potential to destroy or to nourish. As the first card in the suit of wands, the Ace of Wands represents the fire of creativity and the beginning of new adventures and creative pursuits. The image of a hand appearing from the clouds as if by magic symbolically represents the inspiration of the unconscious. The hand*

appears in the foreground of the card, which is set in solitude, away from civilization, which is represented by the castle in the far background. This card represents energy, ambition, and drive and in this sense is similar to the Chariot. There are inspiration, potential, and creativity in the Ace of Wands; it marks the beginning of a journey, whether physical, mental, or spiritual. The energy in this card can also signify a restlessness or uncertainty about how to proceed. You may have energy and passion but not yet have a clear outlet for their expression. The ace of any suit typically represents a raw, unexpressed form of energy that portends a future fulfillment and clarification.

Two of Wands

Words: Red cap, red cloak, blossoming wands, small globe, mountains, lush green earth, small houses, lake or ocean, white lilies, red roses.

Phrases: The number two represents a union, the joining together of opposing forces, the coniunctio oppositorum of which Carl Jung wrote. The two thus represents a definition of the energy represented in the Ace. While the Ace of Wands signifies the fiery energy of inspiration, the Two of Wands represents the beginning of clarity, the formulation of the spark of inspiration into an idea which can be carried out. The man in this card is holding a small globe and stands on the roof of a castle, looking out over a vast terrain to the right and an ocean to the left. He understands his ambition and knows what must be done. This symbol indicates the confidence of self-knowledge. You know what your goal is, what your creative process is directing for you, and you are confident in its eventual fulfillment. There is a sense of success and certainty in this card that is only hinted at in the Ace of Wands. This card indicates the beginning of a new adventure or creative undertaking in which you have a great deal of confidence and which you believe in very strongly. The card does not guarantee certain success, but indicates that you have the inner resources to succeed if you follow through and proceed with wisdom and confidence.

Three of Wands

Words: *Golden sky, mountains, green and red cloak, large sea, three ships sailing.*

Phrases: *The number three represents the expression of the merging of opposites symbolized in the number two. Two lovers unite and a third element, a child, is the fruit of their union. This card represents the undertaking of a creative project or goal. It also signifies the change and the challenges represented by this new beginning. Just as having a child is only the beginning of a long lifetime of relationship, the start of a new venture is only just the beginning. Though there is tremendous satisfaction and joy in the initial undertaking, we often mistakenly feel as if we have "arrived" when in fact the journey has just begun. The man in this card stands at the peak of a mountain overlooking his ships as they start out to sea. He is poised and confident of the success of his mission, yet he knows there are many challenges ahead. There is a new beginning here, as in the card of the Fool, yet here there is wisdom and balance that contrast with the naïveté of the Fool. The Three of Wands represents the satisfaction of a new beginning, the start of a creative venture, the laying of the foundations that must be built on in order to achieve the final satisfaction of completion and maturity.*

Four of Wands

Words: *Golden sky, flowered canopy, garlands of flowers, white and red robes, large castle, group of people, large boulder.*

Phrases: *The Four of Wands depicts a celebration outside the walls of a castle. The canopy of flowers on the four wands is similar to the wedding canopy or chuppah of the traditional Jewish ceremony and thus represents a time of fulfillment and satisfaction at the attainment of a goal. The number four is a number of completion, stability, and realization. The pursuit of the creative journey has begun to bear fruit, and early results are now being enjoyed. This card augurs a time of joy and satisfaction in life and represents the personal gratification of a job well done, a goal attained, a vision beginning to be realized. The four indicates a sense of harmony and balance as well as completion, and thus symbolizes a time of peace and joy in life that comes as the result of often difficult and challenging effort. If you encounter this card in a reading, there is cause for celebration! The Four of Wands is one of the most positive cards in the tarot deck and indicates general good fortune, satisfaction, and fulfillment. But realize, as always, that all things are temporal and that there may be challenges ahead.*

Five of Wands

Words: Blue sky, barren earth, five men fighting with blossoming wands.

Phrases: The struggle represented in the Five of Wands does not necessarily imply the end of the satisfaction and joy symbolized in the Four of Wands. Rather, this card represents the challenges presented to any vision or creative effort by the world or by one's competitors. The joys of a wedding are often followed by domestic struggle to define the boundaries of the relationship and to begin to understand one another in greater depth. The initial success of a creative venture or business is often followed by challenges from rivals who sense success and want to partake of it themselves, perhaps even at your expense. The Five of Wands indicates a personal struggle, whether from within or without, and summons you to face the challenges you are experiencing. As in the card of the Devil, where the evil represented can be overcome by persistence and moral courage, the struggles symbolized by the Five of Wands can be overcome in the same way. The card does not indicate that it is time to quit but that it is time to put forth your very best effort in attaining the goals you have set for yourself. What challenges do you face? How can you deal with them constructively and overcome them?

Six of Wands

Words: Blue sky, crowd of people, wreaths of victory, white horse, green cloak over horse, red cape.

Phrases: The Six of Wands, like the Four, represents an achievement or success in the pursuit of a creative venture. However, the Six of Wands contains a more public element of recognition by others in our community for the fulfillment of a creative effort. A struggle has been overcome, the goal has been reached, and it is publicly acknowledged and celebrated. The card depicts a young man with a victory wreath riding a white horse through a crowd of cheering people. The white horse represents strength, purity, and the success of an adventure. The wand held by the rider also has a wreath tied to it. This is one of the most positive cards in the suit of wands because of its implications of success and fulfillment. Yet, as in all the cards, there is much more than meets the eye. In the midst of victory and celebration it is important to remember the turning of the Wheel of Fortune: Nothing is forever, all things are subject to change. The joy expressed in the victorious rider of the Six of Wands should not be expected to remain with us permanently, but we should celebrate, rejoice, and give thanks for this good while it is ours.

Seven of Wands

Words: *Man standing on hill fighting attackers from below, cliff, green earth, blue sky, green shirt.*

Phrases: *The Seven of Wands, like the Five, again presents a struggle after the initial experience of satisfaction and fulfillment. In this case, the character in the card stands at the top of a hill and is challenged from below by opponents seeking to achieve the success and status of the victor. In a sense, this "king of the hill" game is part of the game of life; the creative, successful individual must continually struggle to maintain his or her position at the top. If your vision and creative effort are fulfilled to the point*

where there is public acclaim or acceptance of your success, then you must expect competition and challenge, for others may also desire the same things. This card indicates a challenge that may appear to block the continued success of a venture or creative effort, but which can be overcome by confidence and continual self-improvement. The challenge may again be from within or without, yet regardless of the source, it can be overcome with effort and clarity of purpose.

Eight of Wands

Words: *Blooming wands, river, green earth, small building, hill, blue sky.*

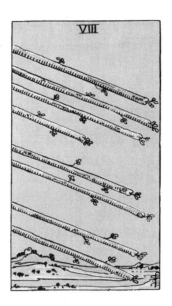

Phrases: *The Eight of Wands depicts eight wands or spears flying through the air in the midst of an idyllic countryside. The flight of wands represents movement, change, and possibly travel. The struggles indicated in the Seven of Wands have been overcome and now the creative journey is nearing its end, coming close to its ultimate completion. The Eight of Wands contains a great deal of energy that propels us toward the fulfillment of our goals. The landscape in the background of the card is lush with greenery and a life-giving river. This card affirms life and the energy required to succeed. Your struggles may be nearing an end and there may be a great deal of change or travel because of the energy and forward thrust of the Eight of Wands. Yet you have the inner resources to deal wisely with the changes brought about by the success of a creative effort, and you are moving steadily forward toward your goals.*

Nine of Wands

Words: *Barren, rocky landscape, red shirt, bandage, all wands in bloom, gray pavement.*

Phrases: *The Nine of Wands depicts a weary, injured man who holds a staff as though in a posture of final defense. He is protected by a number of wands propped up like a wall behind him. This card indicates struggle and the need to call up out of ourselves the strength needed to overcome a challenge that may seem insurmountable. The man in the card has survived many battles and even wears a bandage around his head. Yet in his eye is the determination to overcome this final challenge to his accomplishment and victory. When we encounter the Nine of Wands we are often in the midst of a challenge that appeared just when we thought all was won, at the moment before our final accomplishment of a creative task or goal. The card indicates that we have the inner resources necessary to overcome any difficulty we encounter, even though it may seem impossible at the time. How often do we give up just before we finally achieve success? This card is a sign of hope and encouragement that if we stand firm and strong against challenge, we will achieve our goal. The challenges before us are only the last bit of darkness before the break of a wonderful dawn.*

Ten of Wands

Words: Red clothing, heavy load of ten blossoming wands, blue sky, town, green trees and shrubbery.

Phrases: The Ten of Wands shows a man overburdened with the weight of a heavy load. He walks toward a town like someone who has just gathered harvest and is struggling to bring the fruits of his labors to market. This card, like all others in the tarot deck, has both positive and negative aspects to consider. In one sense, the man is reaping a bountiful reward for hard work in his harvest and thus represents our own success after a long and perhaps difficult struggle. We have realized a dream and must now deal with the consequences of that fulfillment. The attainment of one's goals often carries with it the weight of responsibility, and the Ten of Wands indicates that this weight may be too much to bear. This card represents those among us who are unwilling to let go of excessive responsibility, or those who lose the freshness of the original vision after it has been fulfilled. When a creative venture is begun, as in the card of the Fool, we are lighthearted, carefree, and excited by the new possibilities despite the pitfalls that may lie ahead. In contrast, the Ten of Wands suggests that we have taken on too much and need to release some of the burden. Perhaps this means taking more time out for relaxation and the enjoyment of life, or it may simply mean that we need to adopt a more balanced approach to our worldly cares. Are there unnecessary burdens weighing on you that you can release in a healthy, wholesome way? There is always a need for temperance and balance to maintain psychological and spiritual health.

Page of Wands

Words: *White hat, red bird, flowering staff, barren mountainous landscape, red earth, green shirt, salamanders biting their own tails.*

Phrases: *The Page of Wands is a young man who stands alone in the midst of a barren wilderness, talking out loud about his dreams and desires. He holds his staff in a posture of self-confidence and regal authority and he is well-dressed, healthy, and strong. His shirt is covered with the design of salamanders, creatures associated in mythology with fire and transformation. This young man is very much like the Fool in that he represents change and new beginnings.*

Often the Page of Wands indicates that there is some creative restlessness within us that is anxious for expression, or that we are on the verge of some sort of discovery or new phase of life. The Page of Wands is alone in a barren land, which indicates that much of this creative energy is still very much only a potential, or at best, merely an idea. Yet the Page's radiant energy, the fire of his passion and inspiration, is bursting with the desire for expression and fulfillment despite the fact that no one else is there to hear him. In this sense the Page of Wands represents an early stage of inspiration, or perhaps an immature attachment to a world of dreams that has no basis in reality. The Page of Wands is a call to heed the cries of the unconscious and to follow the creative urge despite the often lonely consequences of being a voice crying out in the wilderness. With persistence and a balanced perspective, even the immature yearnings of the Page of Wands can be transformed into a beautiful and realistic creative vision.

Knight of Wands

Words: *Barren mountainous landscape, pyramids, red horse, flowering staff, silver armor, ragged green shirt, salamanders, fiery plumes.*

KNIGHT of WANDS.

Phrases: *Where the Page of Wands represented the immature beginnings of a new idea or creative adventure that exists only as a castle in the sky, the Knight of Wands represents the active pursuit of that adventure. Since the suit of wands is analogous to the alchemical element of fire, this knight symbolizes the hot passion of inspiration in search of fulfillment. Unlike the Page of Wands, who simply dreams his dream, the knight actively pursues his vision with an abandon that is characteristic of the impulsive astrological sign of Aries. The plumes from his helmet and the decorative tassels hanging from his back and arms are the color of flame, and he, like the page, wears a shirt covered with the symbol of the fiery salamander. His horse is rearing in the intensity of the quest and the knight's face bears the determination of one bound to succeed. However, the negative aspect of this hot pursuit is simply that the Knight of Wands is far too impulsive to see clearly the means of achieving his goal. He sets off on his adventure with the insane determination of a Don Quixote, and his delusions of grandeur will be the cause of much trouble if they're not tempered with reason and balance. When you encounter the Knight of Wands, it is time to begin the journey of creativity with passion and determination, yet this passion must be tempered with a rational, well-considered plan that considers the consequences of any action.*

Queen of Wands

Words: Pale blue sky, greenish-yellow robe, golden crown, flowering staff, sunflower, black cat, sculptures of lions on throne, images of lions and sunflowers on back of throne, barren mountainous landscape.

Phrases: The Queen of Wands represents the aspects of fire that are most important to us. She is warmth, sensitivity, gentleness, and faithfulness as well as strength and determination. The Queen sits on a throne with armrests made of lions, symbols of fire and strength. In her left hand and behind her are sunflowers, which point to life, fertility, joy, and satisfaction. In her right

hand is a wand that is beginning to burst forth with life. In these positive aspects, the Queen of Wands represents fidelity, warmth, and sustenance. However, at her feet is a black cat, a symbol of the darker side of this card. When the Queen of Wands is encountered in a reading it may indicate fidelity, strength, and loyalty, or it may hint at the need for these positive qualities in a situation where they are lacking. Nonetheless, the Queen of Wands is independent and strong, quite able to take care of herself and sustain her own creative vision in the face of potential difficulties. What qualities of this card are relevant to you as you encounter it in your reading?

King of Wands

Words: Blue sky, golden crown, blooming wand, cape and throne decorated with lions and salamanders, salamander crawling along the base of throne, red robe, green cloak.

Phrases: The King of Wands represents the epitome of the qualities we associate with fire. He symbolizes strength, leadership, creativity, vision, and the motivation to bring that creative vision into reality. The King of Wands, like his consort the Queen, holds in his hand a flowering staff of life and creativity. His throne and cape are decorated with both the lion and the salamander, images of fire and strength. The salamanders biting their own tails represent infinity and the ever-present drive to move forward against all obstacles. His robe is bright orange like flame, and his crown has the shape of tongues of fire. The negative aspect of the King of Wands stems from his drive and energy, which can be interpreted by others as aggression, arrogance, or an insolent sense of grandeur. Yet the King of Wands is determined to accomplish his goals at any cost, even if it occasionally causes difficulty in his relationships. On the positive side, this card indicates that you have within you the drive and energy to accomplish your goals if you are willing to look within yourself for inspiration. However, this drive must be balanced with temperance and moderation to avoid the negative consequences involved in the single-minded pursuit of a goal or creative vision.

KING of WANDS

101

Ace of Cups

Words: *Gray sky, ocean, water lilies, mountains, white hand appearing from a cloud, golden chalice, five fountains of water, drops of dew, white dove, wafer or host with a cross on it.*

Phrases: *The suit of cups generally relates to the alchemical element of water and the qualities represented by that element. The Ace of Cups depicts the emergence of spirituality and the awakening of a new awareness of spiritual life. This card contains numerous spiritual symbols. The hand appearing from the clouds represents the emergence of our consciousness of spiritual energy and influence. The hand holds a single cup or chalice, which overflows with five streams of water. The five streams represent the abundance and power of the spirit and the effect of spiritual energy on our five senses. A dove with a wafer or host in its mouth descends from above, signifying the incarnation and appearance of the spirit in the material world. Below the hand is a great sea covered with lotus blossoms, a symbol of the awakening of the human spirit. The Ace of Cups represents newness, rebirth of the spirit, and an awakening of awareness, emotion, and spiritual energy. When you encounter this card in a reading there is an indication of a fresh influx of spiritual and emotional energy in your life, the beginning of a new inner awareness and spirituality that may have been lacking or asleep within you.*

Two of Cups

Words: *Man, woman, two golden cups, green landscape, house, woman wears white and blue, man's shirt is decorated with flowers; green wreath, garland of red roses, winged lion's head, caduceus.*

Phrases: *The Two of Cups represents the union of opposites in its most general sense. The card depicts a man and a woman exchanging cups in a wedding ceremony with the caduceus of Hermes between them. The caduceus has been used since ancient times as the symbol of physicians and healers. The symbol is a staff with two snakes wrapped around it topped by a pair of wings with,*

in this instance, a lion's head between them. The two snakes represent dark and light and their coexistence within us. The wings symbolize the spirit and the lion represents matter and the material world. This card augurs the beginning of a relationship, usually between a man and a woman, although business and other partnerships may be indicated as well. The opposing forces of light and dark, male and female, join together in this card harmoniously, as indicated by the green, verdant hills and the little house in the distance. When the Two of Cups is encountered in a reading, it may not only indicate the beginnings of a relationship but also the need for harmonization of the opposing, often conflicting forces within our own psyche.

Three of Cups

Words: *Three women, one wearing red, one wearing white, one wearing green, three upraised cups, flowers woven into their hair, lush green earth, flowers, fruits.*

Phrases: *The Three of Cups is a card of celebration and accomplishment. The three young maidens dance in a circle with their golden goblets upraised in a toast of joy. The ground is covered with fruit and there is a general sense of abundance and happiness. The number three typically suggests the initial completion of a project or venture and in this case suggests a wedding celebration, the birth of a child, or the successful initial fulfillment of a goal. However, despite the completion or satisfaction offered by the number three, this card also suggests a new beginning; the celebration is only the start of a long and possibly difficult journey. Just as a wedding is both the end of a courtship and the beginning of a lifetime of relationship and commitment, the Three of Cups indicates the celebration of accomplishment that is not only the end of one phase of a journey, but also the beginning of another. When you encounter the Three of Cups there is certainly cause for rejoicing and celebration. Yet you must also prepare yourself for the challenges that may lie ahead.*

Four of Cups

Words: Deep blue sky, lush green earth, large tree, small cloud from which a cup-bearing hand appears, blue mountains, trees, blue tights, red shirt, green vest.

Phrases: The Four of Cups depicts a young man sitting under a tree far away from the city and the commerce of others. His face bears a look of discontent and he is faced with a choice among the four cups before him. His arms are crossed in vexation and indecision and he appears confused and uncertain. The three cups at his feet represent the world and its attractions; the cup appearing from the cloud is the attraction of the spirit and the inner life. This young man and his predicament suggest the story of the Buddha under the bodhi tree, contemplating the state of the universe and unwilling to rise until he has reached the truth. The Four of Cups indicates a time of uncertainty and decision and a turning inward to find the truth for which one is searching. The young man turns his eyes from all the cups, not only the ones representing the world. In this sense, he indicates the need to look deep into oneself to discover the answers one seeks. External influences can be distracting and may not lead us to our goals even if those influences purport to be of a spiritual nature. The young man is involved in the difficult process of individuation Jung speaks of, which can only occur in the solitude of his own spirit. When you encounter the Four of Cups there is a sense that it is time for a reevaluation of your situation and a need to look deep within your own psyche to find understanding.

Five of Cups

Words: *Dark gray skies, river, house or castle, white bridge, green landscape, five cups, black cape.*

Phrases: *The Five of Cups is a card that signifies difficulty, loss, and the challenges of dealing with that loss. The figure in the card wears a black cloak in which he hides his face in apparent despair. At his feet are five cups, three of which have fallen and spilled their contents. The other two, behind his back, remain standing. Ahead of him a powerful river flows between himself and a castle or home in the distance. To his right is a bridge that can lead him to the security of the house across the river. Despite the fact that this card has a strong indication of loss and tribulation, there is a positive aspect that must be considered. Though three of the cups have fallen there are still two that remain, and the bridge in the distance offers the hope of crossing beyond the difficulties being experienced into a land of peace and satisfaction. The Five of Cups indicates a time of challenge and difficulty, the ending of a relationship, or the unsuccessful conclusion or interruption of a creative venture. However, there is always something that remains, always a silver lining behind the clouds. The Five of Cups challenges us to look deeply within ourselves to find the positive aspects of any difficulty we encounter. What is your attitude in the face of such challenges? Is your cup half full or half empty?*

Six of Cups

Words: *Light blue sky, white lilies, blue shirt with a red hood, man carrying a staff, paved walkway, houses, cross.*

Phrases: *The Six of Cups depicts a young boy offering a cup filled with flowers to a young girl. They stand just outside a village, with a quaint-looking house in the background. Five additional cups filled with flowers are placed before and behind the children. This card is a card of sentimentality, nostalgia, and memories of the past. There is something magical in the memory of a happy childhood or pleasant past experiences and this card indicates our desire, in the face of a possibly difficult present, to look back and reminisce about the misty past. However, in this nostalgia for what is gone there is the hope of a new beginning and a better future. Sometimes when thinking about our past we are inspired to project into the future the desires that motivated us back then, and the memory of previously happy times can give us the strength to go forward. Although it is not necessarily always to our benefit to dwell in the memory of the past, occasionally there is joy in those memories and inspiration to proceed confidently into the future. This card is a card of mixed blessings. We should remember good times that have gone but must be careful not to lose sight of the present or to become fearful of the future because we think it might not be as happy as the past. The Six of Cups can be an inspiration to us if we allow the memories of our past to propel us confidently into the future.*

107

Seven of Cups

Words: *Blue sky, gray clouds, black silhouette of a man, blue human head, veiled person with red aura, snake, castle, treasure of colored jewels, wreath and skull, lizardlike creature.*

Phrases: *The Seven of Cups depicts an individual faced with the mysterious appearance of strange images from cups in a floating cloud. Though the character's back is toward us, we can see from the gesture that the apparitions are something of a surprise. The various "prizes" in the cups are a mixture of positive and negative visions, and the character faced with these specters is taken aback by their confusing nature. This card indicates that we are faced with a time of decision, that the images in our minds must be dealt with not only in our dreams but in the world of reality. The character in the Seven of Cups is a dreamer who is able to see beauty and excitement as well as fearful trials and difficulties in the future. If we are constantly caught up in our own dreams, fantasies, and/or fears, we will never be able to move forward and make those dreams reality or overcome those fears. This card indicates that though dreaming is beautiful and provides inspiration for action, we must at some point use those dreams as the stimulus to create our reality. A choice must be made even though the apparent multiplicity of options seems to paralyze us with either fear or excessive anticipation. If you are unable to make a decision because of too many options, it may be time to evaluate carefully the pros and cons of each option and make a thoughtful choice. Castles in the sky are homes for no one, but dreams made real are the fulfillment and expression of our inner creative energy.*

Eight of Cups

Words: Golden moon with human face, deep blue night sky, barren rocks and crags, swampy water, golden cups, man with a staff, red cloak.

Phrases: The Eight of Cups is another card of change and transition. The card evokes an immediate reaction of sadness and a sense of solitude. The young man in this card has turned his back on all he has accumulated or accomplished before. He is disappearing by night into a barren and difficult terrain with only a cloak on his back and a staff in hand. There is a general sense of dissatisfaction from a realization that the things we have fought for and struggled to attain may not be as satisfying as we had hoped they would be. This card resembles the card of the Fool in that the main character is embarking on a journey, yet there are significant differences in the attitude and feeling behind these two cards. The Fool is already at the top of the mountain and is carelessly stepping off the edge. He is naive and inexperienced and the journey he begins is an adventure. The character in the Eight of Cups, on the other hand, has lived and experienced life's joys and sorrows. His journey is undertaken because of a sense of restlessness and unhappiness experienced as the result of achieving all he has desired, yet finding those things to be less fulfilling than expected. This individual has chosen to forsake the familiar and the comfortable in the pursuit of higher goals. He is embarking on a spiritual journey because he has not found deep satisfaction in the things of the world, the things with which he is familiar. If you encounter this card, it is time to ask yourself what you can do to bring a deeper satisfaction and joy to your life beyond the obvious pursuit of material satisfactions and/or physical enjoyments you may have already achieved.

Nine of Cups

Words: *Golden sky and ground, blue curtain, nine golden cups, white garment, bright red hat, crossed arms.*

Phrases: *The Nine of Cups appears to be the very opposite of the Eight. In this card a portly, satisfied man sits with his arms crossed in contentment. Behind him is a wall with nine golden goblets arranged in a structured, well-organized fashion. He enjoys success both materially and spiritually and represents the fulfillment realized after the accomplishment of our deepest desires. Though the meaning appears to be quite contrary to the preceding Eight of Cups, this card can be read in light of its predecessor.*

After the difficult journey of the heart, we are once again able to enjoy satisfaction and joy. The Nine of Cups can therefore represent, on a deeper level, the fulfillment of following the inclinations of our heart and being true to ourselves despite any difficulties that may arise as a consequence. The Nine of Cups indicates a time of joy and satisfaction and the successful accomplishment of our goals and desires. If you encounter this card in a reading there is cause for celebration, as it is generally a very positive card.

Ten of Cups

Words: *Blue skies, family, dancing children, rainbow, river, verdant landscape, house, male characters wearing red, female characters wearing blue.*

Phrases: *The Ten of Cups represents a satisfaction and joy much like that in the Nine of Cups. The difference, however, should be quite clear. The Nine of Cups represents personal attainment whereas the Ten of Cups represents the satisfying fulfillment of a relationship. The card depicts a happy, celebrating family standing together in a field not far from a peaceful and beautiful homestead. The sky is brilliant and clear with the exception of a brightly colored rainbow and the ten golden goblets in it. The Ten of Cups represents satisfaction in a relationship, the satisfaction that is possible only through a deep level of commitment and love. The couple pictured in this card have survived many tests and difficulties and have overcome them all to experience finally a depth of relationship that is rare. The rainbow represents not only happiness and love but also financial stability, prosperity, and the fulfillment of the dreams the couple share. This card is a very positive card in terms of relationships and may indicate either the beginning of a new, very happy relationship, or the ultimate satisfaction of a long-term relationship. Commitment and love are the requirements of such satisfaction, and this card promises that with the required effort a lasting love can be built.*

Page of Cups

Words: *Golden goblet, blue fish, wavy, unstable water, red and blue clothing, white and red roses, blue turbanlike hat.*

Phrases: *The Page of Cups, like the pages in all the suits, represents some sort of beginning or renewal. The young man stands alone at the seashore with a single golden goblet in his hand. Surprisingly, a fish pops its head out of the cup and the young man's face bears a look of curious interest and amusement. The Page of Cups signifies the beginning of creativity or the start of a new project or creative venture. It may also signify the beginning of a new relationship or the dawning of a new perspective on a diffi-*

PAGE of CUPS.

cult situation. The fish, in Christian terms, represents Christ or Christ consciousness. In other mythological systems the fish often represents the unconscious, the spirit, or the life force within us. The Page of Cups indicates the surprising and unexpected nature of inspiration that comes to us from the realm of the unconscious and the spirit. The young man simply expects to raise his cup for a toast or a drink, and instead is confronted with the numinous appearance of a fish, which even appears to be speaking to him. Thus, inspiration is seen to be something that comes on us most unexpectedly and often in a manner that we do not understand. If you encounter the Page of Cups in a spread, it is an indication that there is creative energy trying to burst forth into your consciousness. The unconscious is trying to speak to you, possibly through your dreams or through synchronistic encounters with significant people. The message to be taken is that you must be open to the unexpected, occasionally bizarre impulses of your creative spirit and not shut out inspiration simply because it does not fit in with a rational point of view.

Knight of Cups

Words: Barren mountainous land-scape, winding river, white horse, winged helmet, silver armor, blue and white robe, red fish, golden chalice.

KNIGHT of CUPS.

Phrases: The Knight of Cups repre-sents the undertaking of the creative ad-venture hinted at in the Page of Cups. Whereas the page encounters the mysti-cal fish out of the golden goblet and is thus initially inspired with creativity, the knight has already encountered his inspiration and is about to undertake the journey of imagination and creativ-ity to which the unconscious has impelled him. The knight wears a cloak covered with images of fish, again the symbol of spirit, Christ consciousness, and creativity. His helmet and feet are winged, a symbol of an active and creative imagination. He rides a white horse that walks gracefully under his certain control. The horse represents power, energy, and drive, and of course the color white is a symbol of pu-rity, spirituality, and light. The Knight of Cups represents the power of imagination and inspiration to motivate us to follow the course of creativ-ity and adventure. The knight has heard the call from within and has re-sponded willingly to the challenges of fulfilling his dreams. He rides gracefully into a mountainous, difficult terrain with the certainty that his inspiration will find fulfillment through his efforts and commitment. When you encounter the Knight of Cups in a reading you may need to work on listening more actively to the inner desires and creative urges of your spirit. Or the card may be an indication that you have already embarked upon the adventure of creativity and the search for understanding. The message to be taken then is simply that the road is worth traveling, though there may be difficulties to overcome in the process.

Queen of Cups

Words: *Blue skies, placid body of water, ornate golden cup, small cross, two angel silhouettes, white and blue garb, throne, carvings of cherubs, scallop shell, golden crown.*

Phrases: *The Queen of Cups is the queen of the realm of emotions. She is a beautiful, introspective woman who sits on a throne in the midst of the sea. In her hands she cradles a beautiful cup with handles shaped like angels. The cup is closed, an indication that the thoughts of the queen originate from the unconscious, from the depths of her own soul. The throne upon which she sits is decorated with images of sea nymphs, fish, and scallop shells. The sea and fish are symbols of the unconscious mind, and water in general represents emotion, spirit, and feeling. The Queen of Cups indicates a welling up of feelings that may have been hidden or unacknowledged for some time. On the other hand, this card may indicate an overflow of emotion and sentimentality that could be the source of trouble. The woman in the Queen of Cups represents two aspects of the typically feminine quality of emotion: She is both the good mother, lover, wife, and so on, as well as the unfaithful woman who falls into a relationship because she is overwhelmed by feeling and passion. When you encounter this card in a reading you must examine your own emotional state to determine your strengths and weaknesses. Are you unable to accept the emotional side of your nature? Do you repress feelings? Or conversely, are you overly influenced by your emotions? Do you sometimes find yourself in troublesome situations because you acted without considering the consequences? The Queen of Cups is passionate and beautiful, but as in all experiences in life, there must be a balance to bring about mental, emotional, and spiritual health.*

QUEEN of CUPS.

King of Cups

Words: *Plain gray sky, throne, tumultuous ocean, large fish, red ship, blue robe, golden cloak bordered with red, fish necklace, carving of lotus blossom, golden scepter, golden cup.*

KING of CUPS.

Phrases: *The King of Cups, like all the court cards in the suit of cups, represents emotion, creativity, and the unconscious. Unlike the preceding three court cards, however, the King of Cups expresses much more restraint in his emotional state. He is a master of his own feelings, and remains in control of his emotions. Not to say that he represses those feelings and sentiments; on the contrary, the King of Cups represents the balance between the emotions and the intellect. He is a master of compassion and kindness, and his card often indicates strong bonds in a relationship based on temperance and understanding. He sits calmly in the midst of a turbulent sea and wears a necklace with a fish amulet. The fish is the symbol of spirit and creativity and represents, in this card, the balance of the unconscious with the conscious. The King of Cups does not repress his emotions and unconscious impulses but has learned to accept and deal with them in a mature and balanced manner. Behind him on his right, a fish jumps wildly from the tumultuous ocean, and on his left a ship remains steadily anchored. These images signify that the unconscious has been allowed to break through and has been recognized by the king, yet it remains within his power and does not overwhelm him. When this card is encountered in a reading, it is an indication that you must create balance in the realm of the emotions. The King of Cups represents compassion, one of the most powerful and beautiful sentiments of the human spirit. How can we develop a stronger awareness of the unconscious without being overwhelmed by its power? How can we develop a stronger sense of compassion without falling into the trap of sentimentality?*

Ace of Swords

Words: *Barren landscape, gray cliffs, water, gray sky, gray clouds, white hand, upraised sword, golden crown, drops of golden dew, olive branch, palm branch.*

Phrases: *The suit of swords corresponds symbolically to the alchemical element of air, the most ethereal element of the four. In this sense the swords represent the mind, the intellect, and rationality. In addition, the swords represent power. Thus their two-edged appearance; intellect and power can be used for either good or ill and must be balanced by spirit and feeling. The aces of all suits typically represent new beginnings or the*

inspiration of a new idea or feeling. The Ace of Swords augurs a new understanding of some issue that has been of concern, or the dawning of a new worldview in the broader sense. The barren, mountainous landscape below the sword reflects the often cold nature of intellect. This card indicates the eruption of a new point of view, the inspiration of discovery or intellectual accomplishment. If you encounter this card in a reading, there is an indication that your intellectual life is either receiving too much or too little attention. Though there is great value in the inspiration and power of the mind, intellect must be tempered by compassion and spirit for its true value to be manifested. The two-edged sword cuts deeply in either direction, and a fine line must be walked to achieve the balance necessary for a healthy life. The Ace of Swords is a card of great power and is thus a sign that temperance may be necessary.

Two of Swords

Words: Blue night sky, water, barren islands, stone bench, blindfold, white cloak, two upraised swords, crossed arms, crescent moon.

Phrases: The Two of Swords depicts a young, blindfolded woman who holds a long sword in each hand. She is sitting before a sea filled with rocks and crags that are obstacles to clear passage for ships. This is a card of choice, of the difficulty of decision. The woman in this card is intentionally blinding herself in avoidance of a very difficult choice that must be made. Her avoidance brings her what appears to be a certain peace of mind, for she is very calm and seems somewhat relaxed despite the difficulty of her situation. Occasionally when we are faced with difficult choices we attempt to hide from them and pretend to ourselves and others that if we ignore them long enough they will go away of their own accord. However, the decision will not leave us simply by our willing it to depart; the attempt to play at ignorance is not bliss. Our conscience will eventually force us into facing our refusal to deal directly with the situation. If you encounter the Two of Swords in a reading, there is the general indication that you are faced with a decision and that perhaps you are in a state of denial about the importance of your choice. Life's decisions are frequently quite difficult and raise the possibility of painful consequences, yet not to decide at all is a decision in itself. We must make our decisions confidently and with the best intentions, fully aware of the possible consequences. The avoidance will ultimately lead only to a greater conflict in the end.

Three of Swords

Words: *Gray sky, gray clouds, pouring rain, bright red heart, three shining swords.*

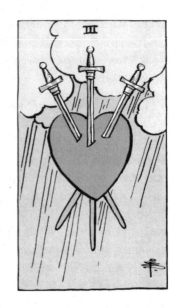

Phrases: *The Three of Swords is a very simply illustrated card with a very difficult message. A heart, suspended in the air, is entirely pierced by three swords. The sky is heavily clouded and rain pours down violently. This card practically speaks for itself; it is a card of loss and difficulty, of sacrifice and broken relationships. It follows upon the difficult decision required in the Two of Swords, where we are avoiding the necessity of making a tough choice. In the Three of Swords, the choice has been made, and we are now experiencing the consequences of our action. Often our choices involve choosing one good over another, or one evil over another, and thus when we've finally made our decision we are still left with the pain of losing the option we have not chosen. Frequently, however, the pain of losing something we once valued (such as a comfortable relationship in which we are no longer growing) is necessary in order to prepare us for a more fulfilling experience in the future. In this sense the Three of Swords is similar to the Death card; we are experiencing the pain of a loss or death of something that may have been important to us but that may no longer be in our ultimate best interests. The positive side of this difficult card, then, is simply that the pain of loss is always followed by a rejuvenation and a rebirth. A reawakening of our spirit will always be experienced if we are able to survive the darkness of difficult times.*

Four of Swords

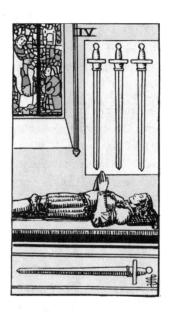

Words: Golden tomb, effigy of a knight in prayer, sword emblazoned on the side of the sarcophagus, three swords hung along the wall in the background, brightly colored stained glass window.

Phrases: The Four of Swords depicts a knight lying on a tomb. His hands are clasped in the position of prayer and the tomb is clearly inside a church. The stained glass behind the statue depicts a woman and child together, and three swords hang from the wall behind the tomb in addition to the one affixed to the side of the bier. This card, contrary to what might be its initial indication, is not a card of death. Rather, it is a card of solitude and the need to experience time apart from others to gather one's thoughts and feelings. Following upon the painful image of the Three of Swords, the Four of Swords indicates our need to spend time alone to reevaluate our lives and situations. Solitude, although often difficult to bear, is necessary for us to be able to reinvigorate our bodies and spirits. Despite the fact that we often desire to get out into the world and interact with others to get our minds off our troubles, sometimes it is more beneficial to us to find a place apart and spend a little time by ourselves. This solitary experience always bears fruit in an experience of greater inner strength and confidence. If we are able to face ourselves directly and not run away from our difficulties we will ultimately become more alive and more aware of the good in our lives, and we will develop the inner strength necessary to cope more readily in the future.

Five of Swords

Words: *Tumultuous blue sky, gray clouds, three men, red shirt, green cloak, mountains, ocean, five swords.*

Phrases: *The Five of Swords is a card representing ambition in a negative sense. Too much ambition without regard to the consequences to oneself or others results ultimately in a situation of loss for everyone. The primary figure in this card is a young man with a look of contempt on his face as he stares at his conquered enemies. He possesses five swords, most of which he has obviously taken from the other characters in the card. The other two figures walk away from him slowly, with an apparent sense of sadness and loss. You, the seeker coming to the tarot for understanding, may be represented either by the callous winner or the dejected losers. In any case a negative connotation is encountered. If your focus is solely on winning your goals at any cost, you will eventually discover to your own dismay that the price of winning may not have been worth the reward. If, on the other hand, you have been defeated by another in a competitive situation, you feel the inevitable sadness of loss. The background of this card is cloudy and stormy, an indication of the turmoil and unrest caused by an uncaring competitiveness. On the positive side, if you encounter this card in a reading you may be ready to change or to accept the difficulty of loss. If you find yourself acting too competitively, you may need to temper your ambition with compassion and an understanding of the consequences to others. If you have experienced loss, you may simply need to accept the loss and let go of what you thought was important to you so you can move forward into a more positive future. Often we value things that are not in our best interests, and forcible loss may be a blessing in disguise. In either case, a new, more balanced attitude may be needed.*

Six of Swords

Words: *Gray evening sky, water, trees, hills, small red boat, veiled woman, small child, swords propped up in boat.*

Phrases: *The Six of Swords appears to project a somewhat sad, melancholy feeling. However, there are both positive and negative aspects to this card, as for any other card in the tarot deck. The card depicts a woman and a young child being ferried across a body of water toward a land just in the distance. Is the ferryman the woman's husband or simply a hired hand? In any case, the woman's head is covered, indicating sadness or loss as she moves away from something in her past. The water to the right of the boat is turbulent, but the water to the left and near the land to which they are journeying is calm and steady. Although there is an indication of change or loss in this card, and therefore a sense of moving away from something, there is also a sense of moving toward a new life. The waters in the distance are calm, and we are moving away from turmoil and conflict toward peace and tranquility. There are times when we are forced to let go of something to which we may have been attached, and the process of letting go is frequently quite difficult. However, the sadness of the loss will ultimately be replaced by greater clarity; the calmness of the water in the distance will bring about a new understanding and a new acceptance of the changes in our lives. Often what seems to be sadness or loss is actually the challenge of a transition to a brighter future and a more peaceful experience of life.*

Seven of Swords

Words: Golden sky, man sneaking away with his arms full of swords, campsite with tents, flags posted on the tops of tents, group of people, barren and fruitless landscape.

Phrases: The Seven of Swords depicts a man escaping from a military camp with a bundle of five swords in his arms. Two other swords remain planted in the ground just behind him. His expression exhibits a sense of overconfidence and mocking, as though he feels absolutely sure of his success. In the distance a small group of soldiers can be seen to the left of the thief; one of them holds a sword upraised. This card is a card of deception and betrayal. The thief is insolent in the confidence of his success, yet the soldiers in the distance may be well aware of his actions. His overbearing self-assurance may cause him to be careless, and he may be caught if he is not extremely careful. This card indicates the difficulty in life of trying to get away with something. Often when we do something in secret, thinking we are safe and undiscovered, something goes awry and our secret is revealed to our embarrassment. The card therefore augurs caution and circumspection when attempting to use cunning to gain an advantage. There is no question that there are times in life when it is necessary to act shrewdly or do something in secret, yet it is these times when our conscience must be particularly active. In the long run, deception does not produce the reward we desire and may in fact cause much damage to our relationships and reputation. If you encounter the Seven of Swords in a reading, it is an indication that caution and wisdom are necessary in the face of a temptation to achieve gain by dubious means.

Eight of Swords

Words: *Blindfolded and tied woman, red dress, swords stuck in the ground, barren and rocky landscape, water, castle, craggy mountain, dull gray sky.*

Phrases: *A woman is exiled from her home, tied up, blindfolded, and surrounded by swords, which act as a kind of prison or enclosure. She stands in the midst of a barren, watery wasteland far from the town or castle in the distance. The sky is gray and cloudy above her and there seems to be no possibility of escape. The Eight of Swords portrays a dilemma much like that experienced in the Two of Swords. We are again faced with the dif-ficulty of a painful decision and we are at an impasse, uncertain which way to go. However, unlike the Two of Swords which forces the choice upon us, the Eight of Swords bases a decision on our own actions. This card fol-lows naturally upon the Seven of Swords, which is a card of duplicity. If we use deception for our gain, ultimately we will be faced with the difficulty of dealing with that deception. However, despite the fact that we may have created a predicament for ourselves, there is a way out. The solution is sim-ply to deal with the situation in the most direct yet tactful manner possible, and face our choice with inner strength. We must be aware of the conse-quences of our actions in all aspects of life, and if we are able to deal hon-estly with ourselves and others, we won't find ourselves in this kind of situation. However, if we are here already, there is still the possibility of freedom from the bondage of our own fears and uncertainties. If you en-counter the Eight of Swords in a reading, it is time to be honest with your-self and others in order to be free of the burden of fear or guilt.*

123

Nine of Swords

Words: *Man clothed in white, hands covering his face, deep black wall, nine swords mounted upon the wall, reddish bed, carving of two men in a sword fight, quilt with blue sections bearing astrological symbols and yellow sections with red roses.*

Phrases: *The Nine of Swords depicts a person who has woken up fearfully from the midst of a nightmare. Nine swords hang on the wall behind him and the base of the bed is decorated with a carving of a duel in which one person is being defeated by another. The quilt covering the individual is decorated with roses and the outlines of astrological symbols. This is the card of fear and nightmares, and therefore has an apparently negative connotation. However, the troubles portended by the Nine of Swords are primarily of a psychological nature and do not necessarily indicate suffering in our external reality. Our experience of the world is greatly influenced by our expectations, desires, and fears. In large measure we are the creators of our own world, and our attitudes determine how we experience that world. The Nine of Swords indicates the paralyzing nature of our fears and negative expectations. If we allow ourselves to be bound by fear of the future we may eventually create a negative reality for ourselves by virtue of our expectations. Thus, the Nine of Swords is a card that expresses an inner reality that may be crystallized or manifested in the external world if we are not able to overcome the negative feelings that affect us. The message of this card is that although all of us experience fear, frustration, and uncertainty, we should not allow those negative emotions to immobilize us or keep us from pursuing our goals with enthusiasm and hope. The future will always be uncertain, yet we can face this uncertainty with inner strength and the support of our higher powers.*

Ten of Swords

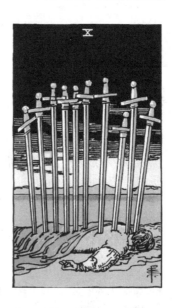

Words: Black sky, golden dawn, blue mountains, dead man facedown, pierced by ten swords, red cloak, barren and empty terrain.

Phrases: The Ten of Swords depicts one of the most painful and sad images in the entire tarot deck. A man lies facedown with ten long swords embedded in his back. The sky above is pitch black and the general feeling is one of sadness, loss, and misfortune. However, despite these ominous images, there are positive aspects to this card. The sea before which the body lies is glassy and calm, and the sunrise is appearing in the distance beyond the mountains. The clouds of darkness are being burned away by the fire of the sun as it rises, and the darkness will soon be dispelled. The Ten of Swords is very similar to the Death card of the major arcana. It is not to be taken literally as an indication of an actual death but rather as evidence of an impending change that may be difficult to accept initially. The Nine of Swords suggests that there is finally closure to an outstanding issue or challenge. This is a card of endings and possibly loss, but as with all endings there is heralded a new beginning, a rebirth, and a rejuvenation of the spirit. We may have been struggling with a difficult decision for some time, or we may have been clinging to something that was ultimately not in our best interests, and now we must learn to let go. The process of change is often difficult, yet life is filled with uncertainty; the only constant in life is change. The Ten of Swords portends a difficult experience of loss or release, but the pain of this experience will eventually be followed by a new awareness and a positive sense of relief that the difficulty is finally past. Though this card may seem negative at first glance, it is a card of hope and an indication that our troubles will not be permanent.

Page of Swords

Words: *Young man, rocky green landscape, bright blue sky, white clouds, ten birds flying overhead, windblown, rough seas.*

Phrases: *The Page of Swords depicts a young individual, probably a young man, standing in the midst of rough terrain with a sword held in both hands. The sky is filled with turbulent clouds and the trees in the background are obviously windblown, as is the young man's hair. The waters behind the youth are rough, and the general sense of this card is one of tumultuous energy. The swords, as we have seen in the Ace of Swords, represent the air, and thus correspond to the ethereal nature of the mind and intellect. This card indicates the turbulent nature of intellectual discovery and inspiration unchecked by experience or wisdom. The page seems to be either on the defensive, hence protecting his ideas, or on the offensive, looking for some victim of the double-edged sword of his mind. Perhaps he is seeking a confrontation in the intellectual sense or has the desire to prove himself mentally superior to others. It is as though the page seeks to embrace an argument for the sake of the mental challenge of this kind of encounter. However, there is also an indication that the page may be inspired with a creative idea and is seeking some means of manifesting this fresh idea in the world. Thus, the Page of Swords represents the turmoil and excitement of fresh thinking and intellectual discovery. If you encounter the Page of Swords in a reading, there is the general indication that you are either experiencing, or on the verge of experiencing, the stimulation of new ideas or discoveries that may inspire you to action.*

Knight of Swords

Words: Bright blue sky, tumultuous clouds, windblown trees, white horse, up-raised sword, deep red cape, helmet with red plume, blue horse's collar, golden butterflies, desolate and empty land-scape, red and yellow earth.

Phrases: The Knight of Swords is a young man who rides a powerful white horse into battle. The sky behind him is filled with storm clouds and the trees are tossed wildly by the wind. The horse's harness is decorated with images of but-terflies and birds and the knight's cape is also decorated with birds. He charges for-ward with fury and apparently without regard to the dangers he may experience.

KNIGHT of SWORDS.

The knight of Swords augurs the action and energy that follows upon the initial inspiration of the Page of Swords. The knight is a fireball of energy and forward momentum, and may indi-cate the beginnings or initial stages of a creative venture, new relationship, or business. The horse seems to ride the wind as its hooves barely touch the ground. The white color of the animal symbolizes the purity of the intellectual energy that motivates the rider. This pure mental energy is a powerful influence, yet without temperance and a realization of the conse-quences of blind action one may become entangled in difficult situations. The knight rides alone, yet he seems ready to encounter a veritable army of resistance. When we are possessed by a pure idea, and wish to manifest that idea in reality, we are often so blinded by the desire for its fulfillment that we fail to see the difficulties we may encounter or the consequences for which we may be responsible. The Knight of Swords is a powerful figure full of life and energy who needs to be balanced with a realization of responsibility and compassion. Pure intellectual energy is a double-edged sword that has the potential for either great good or great evil, and this power must be tem-pered with feeling and spirit to prevent it from creating pain for ourselves or others.

127

Queen of Swords

Words: *Bright blue sky, single bird flying overhead, calm, low clouds, trees, golden crown in the shape of butterfly wings, single upraised sword, gesture of benediction, decorated throne, butterfly, two crescent moons, cherub's face.*

QUEEN of SWORDS.

Phrases: *The Queen of Swords sits on a throne decorated with butterflies and cherubs. Her crown is made of golden butterflies and her robe depicts the sky. Storm clouds gather on the horizon, and the trees in the distance, though somewhat blown about by wind, are much calmer than the trees in the Page or the Knight of Swords. The queen holds a single sword in her right hand, and her left hand is raised in a gesture of benediction or greeting. The Queen of Swords represents the sternness of a mature intellect that is devoid of emotion. Mythologically, emotion is usually a feminine characteristic, yet in this card the woman is stern and composed, obviously without much feeling. This card represents the intellect's ability to judge and discern impartially, without the influence of subjectivity or sentimentality. This card follows upon the rashness of the Knight of Swords, who lets his intellectual energy lead him into precarious situations. The queen represents the calm energy of unbiased intelligence that is able to make judgments based on a careful consideration of all the facts involved with those decisions. She is not swayed by the excitement of new ideas, but is able to consider those ideas and determine the value of them apart from any sense of enthusiasm about the possibilities inherent in them. The Queen of Swords thus represents clarity of thought and judgment. Yet this unaffected mental energy can often be cold and unconcerned with emotional issues. If you encounter this card in a reading, there is the general indication of a need for careful consideration of pending decisions. Yet this intellectual consideration must be tempered by spirit and feeling in order to make the best decision. Pure intellect can be barren of humanity if it is not balanced by compassion.*

King of Swords

KING of SWORDS.

Words: Calm blue sky, clouds, two birds flying overhead, blue robe, red cape, barren landscape, trees, golden crown, back of the throne decorated with butterflies and two crescent moons, upraised sword, small ring on king's left hand.

Phrases: The King of Swords, unlike the characters in the other court cards in this suit, faces us directly from his throne of command. He has a large two-edged sword in his right hand, and his left hand (which has a ring of power on one finger) rests calmly on his lap. The back of his throne is decorated with butterflies, crescent moons, and an angel just near his left ear, positioned as though giving him guidance. The sky is relatively clear with a few peaceful clouds, unlike the stormy weather in the other court cards in the suit of swords. The trees in the background appear motionless and reflect the stern judgment of the king. This ruler is the epitome of intellectual power and represents authority, command, and rulership. His character indicates the leadership of a magistrate, lawyer, or military commander whose emotions must be kept in check under the pressure of battle. There is a sense of fairness about him, however, and his stern appearance is not an indication of brutality. On the contrary, he is the companion to the calculating and shrewd Queen of Swords, and both of these characters represent pure intellect devoid of emotion but impartial in administering justice. The ruler depicted in this card is utilitarian and makes his decisions based on a cold consideration of the facts and the laws for which he is responsible. He follows this law, nearly to the letter, and at times this blind adherence to principles and precepts may preclude the more human aspects of compassion for the circumstances of others. The mind of the King of Swords is cold and razor-sharp but must be tempered by balance with its complementary aspects, emotion and spirituality, for it to achieve its fullest expression.

Ace of Pentacles

Words: *Gray sky, cloud with a single hand, large golden coin or pentacle, lush earth, white lilies, green archway, earthen path, blue peaks, mountains.*

Phrases: *The Ace of Pentacles, like the aces of the other suits, represents new beginnings, fresh energy, and inspiration. The pentacles are analogous to the alchemical element of earth, and therefore symbolize the material world and things associated with matter and the body. Pentacles also represent money and the financial concerns we may have at the time of our reading. The card depicts a single hand with a pentacle coming out of the clouds, very much like the aces of*

ACE of PENTACLES.

the other suits. And, like the other aces, the landscape below the "hand of heaven" represents the primary element of the suit. In the Ace of Pentacles, the landscape is a rich garden with flowers, shrubs, a flowing creek, and mountains in the distance. The Ace of Pentacles indicates the beginning of new energy and revitalized interest in the material or financial areas of your life. This card may represent the beginning of new investments or the willingness to undertake a new business venture. There is also the possible indication of a legacy or influx of money from an unexpected source. The Ace of Pentacles heralds a feeling of prosperity and abundance and should be accepted joyfully; it is a very positive card in general. However, as with any card in the tarot deck, this meaning should not be taken strictly literally. It does not necessarily point to an actual upswing in your financial situation, but it may symbolize a new attitude toward your current position. If you encounter the Ace of Pentacles in a reading, there is an indication of prosperity, fruitfulness, and joy in your life that stems from an inner reassurance of personal well-being and financial stability.

Two of Pentacles

Words: *Light blue sky, tumultuous sea, two ships, red clothing, red hat, green shoes, two golden pentacles, large green lemniscate.*

Phrases: *The Two of Pentacles pictures a man dancing and juggling with a pentacle in each hand. A cord or rope is wrapped around the pentacles in the shape of the symbol of eternity, and in the background two ships are tossed on a stormy sea. The man seems to have a somewhat concerned look on his face, yet he dances with apparent abandon despite the turbulence of the sea behind him. This card follows upon the initial energy of the Ace of Pentacles in which we are psychologically prepared to embrace success and prosperity. The two of any suit typically represents the conflicts inherent in the opposites, and any pending decisions that must be made. In the Two of Pentacles, we find an individual whose consciousness, represented by the waters, is tossed by ostensibly conflicting interests. For example, if the Ace of Pentacles represents the beginnings of a new business or financial venture, the Two of Pentacles represents the need to balance that venture with other important areas of life such as family, friends, and even our own physical, mental, and spiritual well-being. This card indicates the necessity for balance between opposing desires and interests. Though it is necessary to take such circumstances seriously, the Two of Pentacles nevertheless indicates that our psychological health may ultimately be better served if we are able to temper our seriousness and drive for success with a sense of humor and the childlike ability to enjoy ourselves despite our outward condition. The sea of our lives will always be uncertain, yet if we can produce balance and harmony among all the demands on us we will ultimately live happily and in prosperity.*

131

Three of Pentacles

Words: *Interior of a church or cloister, three arches supported by a column, three pentacles carved in the topmost arch, chisel and hammer, two monks, blueprint for construction.*

Phrases: *The Three of Pentacles depicts a mason working in a cathedral. Two monks (or a monk and a nun) hold drawings for him and they appear to be discussing the progress of the building project. The Three of Pentacles, like the threes in the other suits, represents the initial completion of a goal or plan. In this case, it seems to imply the fulfillment and manifestation of a creative venture, business, or building project. The inspiration of the One of Pentacles is beginning to be realized in the material world, and the decisions of the Two of Pentacles have been made successfully. An initial satisfaction is now being enjoyed and the project is well under way. However, this card does not indicate the final completion of any project or venture but rather just the beginning. The number three signifies the first manifestation of a creative union, the* coniunctio oppositorum *of which Carl Jung wrote. Just as a child is born to the union of two lovers, the creative idea is finally born when the conflicting desires of the heart are in equilibrium and when fear of failure is balanced with enthusiasm for potential success. The message of the Three of Pentacles, therefore, is primarily one of encouragement. If you continue to work toward the fulfillment of your dreams and do not allow disillusionment to dampen your enthusiasm, ultimately you will experience prosperity and success in your goals. What new beginnings are you experiencing in the material realm? Is there some project or creative venture you have been putting off because of fear of failure? The Three of Pentacles indicates that dreams can be made real with persistence, determination, and effort.*

Four of Pentacles

Words: Large city, red robe, black cape, golden crown, bland and colorless gray sky, gray throne or seat.

Phrases: The Four of Pentacles shows a man sitting on a stool apart from a town that we assume is his own. He is crouched tightly and holds his pentacles or coins in a very defensive posture, as though he were hoarding them for fear of loss. His eyes appear darkened from hard work but his mouth betrays the hint of a smile that comes from the self-satisfaction of his accomplishments. The Four of Pentacles indicates one of the dangers of prosperity: the temptation to value money far above its real worth. If wealth and financial success lead to miserliness or an ungenerous attitude, then our psychological energy is in a closed or contracted state wherein nothing is perceived to have value other than money. This attitude is, of course, an expression of extreme attachment to the things of this world and is unhealthy in the long run simply because it is such an extreme point of view. Though the Four of Pentacles can be a herald of material gain and/or success, it must nevertheless be tempered with a realization that money is simply a means of exchange, a method we use to assign value or to express our opinion of the value of things. In itself it is actually worthless, yet as a measure of our own self-worth it can be very powerful. However, it is always a mistake to measure one's worth solely on the basis of the amount of money one controls. The Four of Pentacles is a warning to be careful about the pitfalls inherent in your relationship to money. If you encounter this card in a reading, it may indicate a coming financial success. It may also be a sign that your feelings about money may be somewhat imbalanced. The fear of losing what we already have may itself prevent future gains. How does the image of the miser in this card speak to you?

Five of Pentacles

Words: *Dark evening light, snow falling, snow on the ground, two beggars, ragged, torn clothing, stained glass window, church, tree with five pentacles in its branches.*

Phrases: *The Five of Pentacles, like the fives in the other suits, portrays a situation of adversity. Again, as with any card in the tarot deck, the meaning of this card should not be taken completely literally. Here we encounter a destitute couple walking through the snow outside the stained glass of a church window. The man uses a crutch because of his crippled leg and the woman attempts to cover herself with her threadbare shawl. The Five of Pentacles may literally augur a time of financial strife and this possibility must be considered. However, other meanings of this card may surface, depending on your psychological state at the time of the reading and your attitudes and expectations about money. Just as the Four of Pentacles indicated a psychological attachment to money and a tendency to overvalue it, the Five of Pentacles is also likely to indicate an inner difficulty with your relationship to money and material things. This card may therefore indicate a lack of confidence that is reflected in your self-judgment. If money becomes the primary motivating force in life and the gauge by which we judge our worth, the lack of it may produce anxiety and a sense of being excluded from the good things money can provide. In addition, if we encounter financial difficulties such as the loss of employment or an investment gone sour, we may fall into the trap of losing faith in our ability to re-create a positive financial situation for ourselves. If you encounter the Five of Pentacles in a reading, you should not only consider your actual financial circumstances but also your attitudes toward money. What fears do you experience about money? Is there anxiety that there will never be enough, or do you have faith in your ability to manifest what you need to live a prosperous, fulfilled life?*

Six of Pentacles

Words: *Six floating pentacles, gray sky, wealthy merchant, red overcoat, scale, two beggars, yellow robe, blue robe, trees, white buildings.*

Phrases: *The Six of Pentacles depicts a wealthy merchant distributing some of his wealth among the poor outside the walls of a town in the distance. In his left hand he holds a small scale, indicating that his philanthropy is executed with justice and fairness. The beggars gladly accept the coins he is distributing among them. This card appropriately follows the difficulties of the Five of Pentacles. In the Six of Pentacles, you as the questioner may be represented either by the rich merchant or by the beggars at his feet. In any case, there is a sense of peace and happiness about this card because it indicates the ending of tribulation. The merchant represents not only the attainment of prosperity and financial stability, but also the experience of psychological peace in your relationship to money. The generous person has truly understood the value of money as something which can and should ultimately be used for the good of either oneself or others. The beggars, on the other hand, are blessed by the unexpected occurrence of good luck in their difficult lives. In this sense, the Six of Pentacles may foretell the arrival of good fortune and the end of financial woes. The Six of Pentacles reflects a sense of stability and balance, and the ending of a period of financial difficulty. If you encounter the Six of Pentacles in a reading, there is the general indication of good fortune and balance in your financial and material situation.*

Seven of Pentacles

Words: *Melancholy man, rake or shovel, gray sky, gray and barren land, large vine or plant, pentacles growing from plant.*

Phrases: *The Seven of Pentacles portrays a young man taking a rest from the difficult work of harvesting his abundant crop. He gazes meditatively at the pentacles hanging from the rich greenery of the thicket in which he works and seems to be contemplating the value of his efforts. This card follows upon the Six of Pentacles, which indicated the ending of a difficult period of financial or material difficulty. In the Seven of Pentacles, the situation is completely reversed and we now experience the rewards of hard work and effort. However, there is a decision looming in the air and this choice is at the root of the young man's contemplative expression. The question at hand is simply whether the rewards of hard work are in fact worth the effort to acquire them. It is often at the time of our greatest success that we realize what we desired so strongly is in fact somewhat disappointing. This card also indicates the need to reevaluate our goals as we work toward their accomplishment. Sometimes our initial vision of a project or creative venture undergoes significant change when the reality of that vision begins to take shape. If you encounter the Seven of Pentacles in a reading, you are likely to be experiencing a time of change in terms of your financial situation. You may have already accomplished a great deal, or you may still be working hard to attain success. In either case you must consider the value you place on material abundance. As we saw in the Four of Pentacles, an over-attachment to money ultimately creates negative energy in your life and possibly even the loss of that which you valued so highly. It is time to reconsider your goals and reevaluate them in light of a balanced, healthy perspective that takes the psychological, emotional, and spiritual aspects of life into consideration.*

Eight of Pentacles

Words: Gray sky, tree or column on which are hung a number of golden pentacles, chisel, hammer, white buildings, red tights, blue tunic, black apron or vest.

Phrases: The Eight of Pentacles is the card of apprenticeship. While the seven indicates a time of decision and the reevaluation of our financial situation, this card means that a decision has been made and a new creative venture is under way. An apprenticeship is a time of learning new skills, a time of beginning something that one has not previously done. In this sense, the Eight of Pentacles indicates that you are experiencing or about to experience a change or new beginning in terms of work, education, or financial circumstances. However, unlike many of the other cards indicating change or renewal, the Eight of Pentacles symbolizes a concentrated determination to master a new skill. Some of the cards that augur change seem to imply that the change will be chaotic, unstructured, or forced upon us either by external circumstances or psychological necessity. The Eight of Pentacles represents the single-minded effort of someone who has consciously chosen a new career path or creative undertaking. This card is the herald of success through perseverance and initiative as opposed to luck or the generosity of others, as indicated in the Six of Pentacles. If you encounter this card in a reading and are not currently engaged in the active pursuit of your goals, it may be time to ask yourself what you could study or create to better yourself or your circumstances. If you are already engaged in the pursuit of new learning, the Eight of Pentacles may be a card of encouragement and reassurance that the energy you invest in your apprenticeship is worth your while.

Nine of Pentacles

Words: Woman wearing long red and yellow robe, bird, vineyard, golden pentacles, two trees, hills, house, golden yellow sky.

Phrases: The Nine of Pentacles is a card of prosperity and the solitary enjoyment of one's own accomplishments. The picture is of a mature woman walking in a vineyard. The vines are heavy with grapes and golden coins, representing the fruitful accomplishment of all her desires. A falcon sits calmly on her left hand, symbolizing her own intellectual and spiritual self-control. Far in the background is a large house, presumably belonging to the woman herself. There is

a general sense of peace, satisfaction, and the fulfillment of a creative venture or personal investment in the image of the Nine of Pentacles. Unlike the initial satisfaction indicated in the Three of Pentacles, this represents a more permanent, lasting achievement as the result of one's own efforts. The woman is alone in this image, signifying that the success she enjoys is not based on the opinions or judgments of others. Rather, the pleasure she experiences is the result of persistence and the determination to invest her time, energy, and perhaps even financial resources, into the goals she has set for herself. The most successful individuals are often greatly rewarded by taking risks despite the warnings of naysayers or skeptics who discourage them. The Nine of Pentacles offers encouragement to follow our dreams despite the warnings or negative impressions of others, even those who are closest to us. If you believe in your heart that the goals you set for yourself are achievable and worthwhile, you should not be swayed from pursuing them simply because someone else may not share your vision.

Ten of Pentacles

Words: *Old man, opulent robe decorated with grapes, flowers, and moons; two white dogs, man, woman, child, archway leading to town.*

Phrases: *The Ten of Pentacles is a card of culmination and final fulfillment. The image depicts an aged, wise man sitting comfortably just outside an archway leading into a town. He is surrounded by his family and his dogs and wears a rich robe decorated with images of grapevines, crescent moons, and other symbols. Behind the laughing couple under the arch, a young boy reaches playfully to pet one of the dogs. This card is a symbol of financial security, accomplishment, and comfort. The patriarch is able to rest and enjoy the fruits of his labors in retirement while he looks on at the lives of his children and grandchildren. Here we have someone who has accomplished a great deal during his life and is now able to rest in the satisfaction of knowing that what he has created will provide value and joy to others even when he is gone. The Ten of Pentacles indicates, like the Nine, that effort and perseverance will ultimately provide satisfaction and the joys of creative accomplishment. There may be an indication of financial good fortune and stability in this card, yet much more is implied than simply material success. There is a sense of mental, emotional, and spiritual stability suggested in the Ten of Pentacles as well as the material, financial success that is obviously indicated by the image. If you encounter the Ten of Pentacles in a reading, you are likely to be experiencing a time of lasting fulfillment as the result of your own efforts and hard work. The card may also be a source of encouragement to continue following your dreams and working toward the accomplishment of your inner vision.*

Page of Pentacles

Words: *Golden yellow sky, young man, green tunic, red turbanlike head covering, green landscape, cluster of trees, flowers, blue mountain.*

PAGE of PENTACLES.

Phrases: *The Page of Pentacles is a young man who stands alone in a field full of freshly blossoming flowers. Behind him in the distance to his right is a grove of lush trees, probably fruit-bearing, and to his left lies a newly furrowed field that promises an abundant harvest. The page walks slowly as though he were unaware of anything around him other than the golden coin that seems to float in his hands. The Page of Pentacles, like the pages of all the suits, is a card of new be-*

ginnings, of inspiration and the initial stages of a creative project or venture. The young man is absorbed by the coin in his hands, which represents his goals and dreams. Pentacles correspond to the alchemical element of earth, and in this sense the coin may symbolize the beginnings of sensual awareness not only in terms of money and its value, but also in terms of a growing awareness of the importance of health and other material needs. The Page of Pentacles is a card of dreams and the desire to fulfill those dreams in the material world. If you encounter this card in a reading, there is an indication that you may be in the midst of a new undertaking such as a hobby, business venture, or the beginning of a new educational experience. In any case, the page is a sign of enthusiasm and desire. He does not indicate the fulfillment of dreams as much as the initial motivation and energy to begin the process of creating those dreams in reality. This is a card of encouragement; castles in the air may be beautiful in theory, but now is the time to begin to put foundations under them.

Knight of Pentacles

Words: Black horse, suit of armor, green plume on helmet, red cape, red rolling field, trees.

KNIGHT of PENTACLES.

Phrases: The Knight of Pentacles, like the knights of the other suits, represents work, effort, and the responsibility that follows upon the dreams of the page. Whereas the Page of Pentacles walks sleepily through a fertile field, the Knight of Pentacles sits on a heavy plow horse in the midst of that same field. In his hands he carries a single gold coin, but his eyes reflect careful thought and consideration rather than the dreamy gaze of the page. The knight is engaged in the often toilsome, routine efforts required to realize the dreams of his heart. He is building the foundations to support the castles the page has built in the air. The Knight of Pentacles, representing work and effort in the material realm, sits quietly on his horse, unlike the knights of the other suits, who ride with careless energy toward their goals. This card is a symbol of care, diligence, and responsibility in the world. The knight is a dedicated, loyal worker who is patient and willing to struggle through boredom and routine if it is necessary to accomplish his goals. If you encounter this card in a reading, there may be an indication that you are deeply involved in working toward the fulfillment of your goals and dreams. If this is not the case, the card may indicate a necessity to plant your feet firmly on the ground in order to manifest your dreams in reality. Again, castles in the air are beautiful, but without foundations below them they are nothing but an illusion of the mind and heart. Perseverance and effort are always required to accomplish anything of value, and the Knight of Pentacles is an example of that patience, which will ultimately be rewarded.

Queen of Pentacles

Words: *White robe, red cloak, golden crown, flowers, blue mountains, canopy of vines and red roses, rabbit, rich and verdant landscape, ornately decorated throne with carvings of rams' heads, fruit-bearing trees.*

Phrases: *The Queen of Pentacles depicts a solitary woman, much like the one in the Nine of Pentacles. However, the queen represents a greater degree of fruitfulness and satisfaction. Here we have the queen of sensual enjoyment, an earth mother similar to the empress of the major arcana. She sits on a throne decorated with carvings of fruit trees, goats, angels, and other symbols of mate-*

rial success and sensual pleasure. The tree above her and the ground beneath her feet are rich with flowers and ripe plants of all sorts and she holds in her hand a single golden pentacle, which represents her material wealth. At the very lower right-hand corner of the card a rabbit, the symbol of reproduction and fertility, darts out from behind some bushes. This card represents the fulfillment of a creative project or the final accomplishment of a dream or goal. We have worked hard to realize our desires, and now we are able to relax and enjoy the fruits of our labors. If you encounter the Queen of Pentacles in a reading, there is an indication that you are experiencing or about to experience the attainment of a long-standing goal toward which you have been struggling. This card may also be a sign to you that the enjoyment of the material, sensual aspects of your nature must be balanced with the mental, spiritual aspects. Anything in the extreme is unhealthy, but a balanced life of temperance and peace produces health, vitality, and personal well-being.

King of Pentacles

Words: *Golden sky, white buildings, throne carved with bulls' heads, cloak decorated with images of grapes and grape leaves, golden crown, golden scepter, red roses.*

Phrases: *The King of Pentacles is the card of worldly success, ultimate fulfillment, material satisfaction, and high ambition. He sits on a throne decorated with carvings of bulls and vines and his robe is covered with embroidered grapevines rich with fruit. At his feet and all around him are vines, flowers, and plants of all sorts, representing the highest attainment of material success.*

In his right hand he holds the scepter of his power and in his left he holds a golden coin, symbolic of his material influence. Behind him is his castle, the symbol of all he has built through his efforts and determination. This card is the representation of the final achievement of a creative task, business venture, or investment. Here we see a king who has reached the pinnacle of his financial power and influence and is able to rest assured of his continued prosperity. He is no longer required to struggle to achieve what he desires, like the page and the knight, and is able to accomplish anything he wants because he has already proved himself. This is a card of self-confidence and certitude. If you encounter this card in a reading it may indicate that you are sure of your abilities and have what it takes to reach your dreams. It may also be a card of encouragement indicating that your goals can be accomplished through perseverance and determination. On the other hand, this card may be a warning to those who have already arrived. As is indicated in all the cards of the tarot deck, there is a need for temperance in all we do. If you are too attached to material or financial satisfactions, other aspects of your life may suffer unjustly. If the ambition or desire for success is so great that family life and relationships are destroyed, the goal of your work may not be as satisfying to you in the end.

TAROT SPREADS

*T*arot readers often draw cards individually to obtain answers to specific questions. For example, many people draw a single card each morning as their "daily card," which might set the tone for the day or offer material for meditation. Or you can draw a single card when seeking an answer to a yes or no question. However, though each individual card contains a wealth of symbolism and meaning, the most common way to work with the tarot is to arrange the cards in a spread and interpret the cards in relation to each other. Spreads are traditional arrangements of tarot cards in which each position represents a specific meaning. As a spread is interpreted, each card is considered by itself in relation to its current position, as well as in relation to the other cards in the spread.

The card layouts described here provide frameworks for in-depth readings of matters relating to your personality and spiritual life. They can also stimulate your creativity by providing ideas for new spreads you can create yourself. Any symbol, pattern, or design can be used as the basis for a tarot spread. For example, you can create a spread based on the symbols of the triangle, the pyramid, the square, or the circle. You can create spreads based on star patterns such as the pentagram or the hexagram. Any symbol, significant shape, number, or image can be used as the basis for a new tarot spread. The traditional spread frameworks offered here should be starting points for your own explorations of the possibilities inherent in the tarot. Just as the interpretations presented in this book for each tarot card should spark your own discovery of meanings, the spreads offered here should be used as inspiration for creations of your own.

The spreads described below are all included on the Cyber-Tarot CD-ROM. An example using the Celtic Cross spread for a reading was provided earlier in the book. A second example, using only the major arcana, is offered in Appendix B at the end of the book. By studying the examples and working with the software, you'll quickly become adept at interpreting tarot spreads for yourself and for others.

CELTIC CROSS CARD LAYOUT

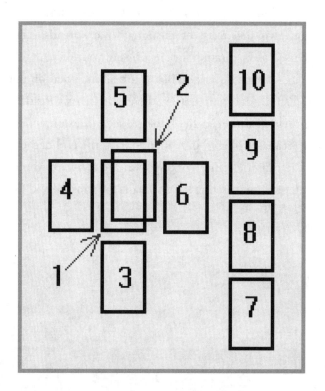

he Celtic Cross spread is probably the most well known and popular layout for reading the tarot. For this reason, it is the default layout of CyberTarot. The Celtic Cross is one of the easiest spreads to work with, yet it is also one of the most powerful and effective. It should be used most often when you are just beginning to work with the tarot. Try some of the other layouts when you are comfortable with this one and feel ready to move into other areas of exploration. However, don't feel that this spread is only for beginners. The Celtic Cross remains the most popular spread because of its power to reveal the depths of the unconscious to the alert reader. The arrangement consists of cards laid out in the shape of a cross with a vertical line of additional cards just to its right.

POSITION NUMBER ONE
The Significator

The first card to be revealed is in the center of the spread and is known as the significator. This card represents you, the seeker, in your current state of mind. It also signifies the issues that are of concern to you in the present time, and the inner influences that affect you.

POSITION NUMBER TWO
The Crossing Card

The second card to be revealed is considered the crossing card and represents that which crosses, opposes, or influences you. This influence can be either positive or negative and must be understood not as a singular force but as part of the overall trend displayed in the reading as a whole.

POSITION NUMBER THREE
The Foundation

The third card appears at the bottom of the cross and represents the foundation or basis for the current question or issue being presented to the tarot. This card signifies the root issue that has brought you to the cards. Often this card reveals issues that lie beneath the surface of your consciousness and that may not be immediately evident or may in fact be quite surprising. It may also represent past issues that are still weighing on your mind.

POSITION NUMBER FOUR
The Recent Past

The fourth card in the spread represents past events, issues, and concerns. This card denotes a situation that is passing or has already passed out of your life. It may be something that was once significant to you and has since lost its urgency, or something you are clinging to and need to let go of in order to move forward into the future.

POSITION NUMBER FIVE
The Crown

The fifth card represents issues that are important in the present or that may come to pass in the future. This card does not predict a fixed and certain future event but rather indicates a possibility you may or may not encounter, depending on how you react to the present situation. The crown position is a bridge between the present and the future and may manifest a significant issue that is in the process of being resolved or that may have implications in the immediate future.

POSITION NUMBER SIX
The Future

The sixth card more clearly represents what lies before you. It may denote the general resolution of issues involved in the crowning card or events that are about to manifest in your life. The card should not be read literally as an absolute prediction of the future as much as a description of psychological and personal trends that will be of significance to you in the times ahead.

POSITION NUMBER SEVEN
Emotions, Feelings

This card signifies your current emotional and psychological state. It is closely related to the significator. Understanding this card together with the first card can provide great insight into your current emotional situation, including your fears, attitudes, and expectations. This card reflects most strongly your inner state at the time of the reading.

POSITION NUMBER EIGHT
External Influences

The eighth card signifies the influence of others in your life. It may reflect their opinions and perspectives about you, or it may reflect what you believe others think of you. This card also represents the way others view you in your current situation and generally signifies trends in your relationships with others.

POSITION NUMBER NINE
Hopes, Ideals, Desires

The ninth card in the layout denotes your hopes and desires for the outcome of the issue at hand. This signifies your inner state and the image you have in mind for the fulfillment of the situation you have come to the tarot to resolve or understand. The card may provide insight into the way your ideals and preconceived notions affect your understanding of the issue.

POSITION NUMBER TEN
The Outcome

The tenth card represents the final outcome or resolution of the issue being brought to the tarot for understanding. Again, it should not be taken literally as a predetermined and fixed future. Rather, it should be considered in context of the entire reading. Frequently the culminating card brings clarity to understanding other cards in the spread that may have been uncertain in meaning. This card should tie the entire reading together and provide the overall theme for the reading.

CHAKRA CARD LAYOUT

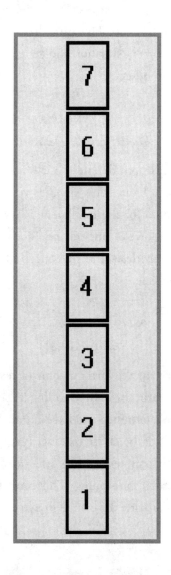

The Chakra card layout has its origins in yoga philosophy. In the chakra system the human body contains seven cardinal points, or chakras, which are arranged along the spine and contain our motivating energies and internal influences. Balancing the energy of the chakras creates psychic, spiritual, and physical equilibrium in our lives. To read a tarot spread in light of the chakra system can give us insight into our own physical, mental, and spiritual condition at the time of the reading and may provide clues to areas in our lives where we need additional energy to create balance and wholeness. The Chakra spread is most beneficial as a tool for understanding oneself, and as a means for gaining self-knowledge. Although future concerns may be revealed by the cards, you should read the spread as a key to your own psyche rather than as an indicator of a predetermined or fated future.

POSITION NUMBER ONE

The Root (Muladhara)

The root chakra is the energy center the primary influence of which is the material, physical level of our being. This circle of energy is most related to the primary issues of our bodies and the lower energies that pertain to fundamental concerns such as basic physical survival. Of all the chakras, the root contains the lowest level of energy. The location of this center is at the base of the spine, just between the genitals and the anus.

POSITION NUMBER TWO

The Sexual Center (Svadisthana)

The second chakra is located at the genital level and represents our sexual energy center. If our energies are blocked or concentrated here, our psychological focus is primarily on the sexual, and we interpret or misinterpret everything in terms of sex. This is not only the reproductive center but also the center of lust, craving, and desire.

POSITION NUMBER THREE

The Power Center (Manipura)

The third chakra is the center of emotions and the desire for power. The energy at this level is primarily concerned with domination and control, although it is also an area of concentration of emotion and instinct. Individuals with a primary convergence of energy at the third level are concerned with accomplishment, achievement, and ambition as well as emotion and feeling in general.

POSITION NUMBER FOUR

The Heart (Anahata)

The first three levels bear the energy of our physical, material manifestation. The level of the heart is the first level where truly spiritual energy is manifested. The fourth chakra is the center of love, not in the sense of sexual love but in the sense of the universal love of the divine. This is the center of openness to others, the center of goodwill and self-giving. It is also the center of the beginning of spiritual awareness.

POSITION NUMBER FIVE

The Throat (Vishuddha)

The fifth chakra represents the gate of psychological and spiritual transformation. It is at this level that our consciousness shifts from attachment to the material realm to an awareness of the undivided unity of the divine. This center is one of transition and represents the search for truth and the yearning for union with truth. This chakra may represent the urge toward self-expression and is also a center of creative energy in that it is the doorway to the world of the spirit.

The Third Eye (Savikalpa Samadhi)

The sixth chakra is the realm of spiritual realization, intuition, psychic abilities, and awareness of the divine. It is not yet the complete union with the all-encompassing energy of the universe, but is a highly evolved spiritual level where individuals are aware of themselves as separate entities who perceive the glory of the One. Thus, the "third eye," centered between the brows, is able to perceive that which was previously unseen.

Ultimate Liberation (Nirvikalpa Samadhi)

The seventh chakra appears at the crown of the head and represents the ultimate spiritual attainment. An individual who awakens this chakra center loses his or her own individuality in the sea of divinity in which everything lives and moves and has its being. The energy at this level is of the incomprehensible light of God, which overwhelms and envelops the individual in the highest state of spiritual awareness.

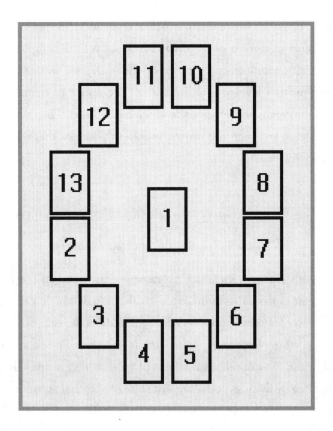

The Horoscope spread is based on the concepts of astrology. The cards are spread in the shape of a circle, with a significator in the center to represent you, much like the significator in the Celtic Cross layout. This spread will be most helpful if you have an understanding of the concepts of astrology, as the correlations revealed by the cards will be more clear if you are familiar with astrological signs and the concept of astrological charts.

The Horoscope layout is particularly valuable in providing insight into your inner workings, your state of being at the time of consultation. It offers great insight into personality and psychological issues and should be read as a guide to self-knowledge rather than a divination of the future, although as in all the spreads, future issues and trends may be revealed by the cards.

POSITION NUMBER ONE

The Significator

This position represents you in the same way that the significator represents you in the Celtic Cross spread. Its meaning encompasses your current state of mind and spirit, and indicates your overall condition at the time of your tarot reading.

POSITION NUMBER TWO

Aries (First House)

The first house corresponds to the sign of Aries, the first sign of the zodiac. This house represents your self, your personality, ego, and temperament, and as such is a strong complement to the significator. The first house can often signify your outward appearance, as well as your mannerisms and behavior. Your interests, attitudes, and desires are also contained under the influence of the first house. The first house represents beginnings, change, and newness.

Taurus (Second House)

The second house represents possessions and financial matters. It, too, is a reflection of your personality, but more in the sense of the external elements that define who you are and the material things that are important to you. This house represents your attitudes toward money and possessions as well as the items themselves, and can thus disclose a great deal about your perceptions and feelings about the material world. The second house can also be an indicator of the ways in which money and material things may be attracted to or repelled from you.

Gemini (Third House)

The third house influences your relationships, particularly with siblings and neighbors. It also governs communications and travel. In this sense, the third house is primarily concerned with your interactions with others. Self-expression is influenced strongly by the third house as is your ability to influence others through written and oral communication. The third house also influences study and learning, intellectual ability, memory, clarity of thought, and creativity.

Cancer (Fourth House)

The fourth house influences your home life, and your relationships to your mother and father. It also concerns your ancestry, and your own aging and later life. This house is very personal in that it relates to everything you consider "home," including your spiritual life and emotions. The primary energy of the fourth house is that of personal domain and everything it means to you.

POSITION NUMBER SIX

Leo (Fifth House)

This house is the center of the heart. It influences love and sexuality, as well as your creative urges and instincts in a more general manner. Children are also under the rule of this house, as are the playthings and imaginative ventures of their young lives. As such, this house also influences the gaming tendencies of adult life, such as the desire for adventures, gambling, and entertainment of various sorts. This is a house filled with feeling and emotion, creativity and excitement.

POSITION NUMBER SEVEN

Virgo (Sixth House)

The sixth house influences two primary areas of your life: your health and your relationships with others, particularly those to whom you can be of service or those subordinate to you in the workplace. This house reflects your desires and attitudes toward serving others and the giving of yourself to the benefit of the world. It also governs your relationships with coworkers and employers. Your physical health is influenced by this house as are your diet and hygiene habits.

POSITION NUMBER EIGHT

Libra (Seventh House)

The seventh house is the house of close relationships and partnerships. Marriage is under the influence of this house, as are other kinds

of agreements and contracts. Partnerships can include business partnerships or other close relationships where joint effort or energy
might be invested in a common goal. The aspect of close partnerships
also includes the negative elements of such relationships and may indicate the influence of rivals or adversaries in your business or creative
life.

POSITION NUMBER NINE

Scorpio (Eighth House)

The eighth house represents the house of death, inheritance, and the
afterlife. It also signifies rebirth and regeneration in a manner similar
to the Death card of the major arcana; death represents endings but
also holds the seeds of new beginnings. This house has a very strong
influence on spirituality and mysticism, and those influenced by the
eighth house often possess strong psychic or spiritual abilities. In addition, this house governs legacies and those things left behind by the
dead, as well as taxes and debts.

POSITION NUMBER TEN

Sagittarius (Ninth House)

The ninth house influences philosophy, higher thoughts, and distant
travels both of the mind and the body. It can be considered an expansion of the third house of study and communication but exists at a
more subtle, elevated plane of thought. This house includes the influence of intuition, education, religion, and spirituality. Travel can include foreign travel or any journeys that would broaden the mind by
the experience of new and unknown things.

TARQT
SPREADS

Capricorn (Tenth House)

The tenth house is the house of profession and career, as well as public life and image in a broader sense. It is the opposite of the fourth house of "home" in that it relates to those aspects of your personality that are publicly known rather than hidden or personal as in your home life. This house includes the opinion others have of you, as well as your material success and your ways of dealing with social responsibilities. The tenth house primarily reflects those elements of your personality that are social rather than private, and material rather than spiritual.

Aquarius (Eleventh House)

The eleventh house influences friendships and social activities, hopes and ideals. The social influence of this house pertains more to those associations to which we attach ourselves for pleasure and camaraderie rather than social duty or obligation. Also under the influence of the eleventh house are our hopes and ideals; often these are reflected in the organizations with which we choose to affiliate ourselves. The friends that come under the influence of the eleventh house are those to whom we feel most strongly attracted because they reflect our ideals and interests and therefore strengthen our attachment to them.

Pisces (Twelfth House)

The twelfth house is the final house of the Horoscope spread and therefore represents the limitations, sorrows, and difficulties in our lives. This house has been associated with one's karma in that it concerns the rewards and punishments for the deeds we have done. It is also associated with things that limit us and governs prisons, hospitals, and anything that serves to bind and restrain us. It also reflects tendencies toward self-undoing, escapism, and self-defeating attitudes that limit us from within. Often this house reveals areas in our lives that can be overcome if faced courageously, and therefore has the positive consequence of potentially being the house of ultimate self-revelation and discovery of the truth about ourselves.

SACRED MANDALA CARD LAYOUT

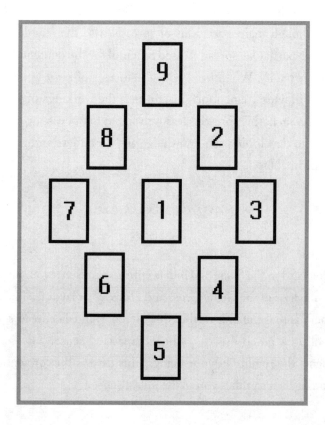

*M*andalas are archetypal forms that are used for meditation and represent the totality or wholeness of the psyche. The mandala has been used as a tool for contemplation throughout the ages in all parts of the world. Often these forms are symmetrical or circular in shape and contain other symbolic images. Well-known mandalas contain images of deities and figures such as triangles and squares that contain significant symbolic meaning. In the Christian tradition, the great rose windows of Gothic churches are mandalas used to express the truths of the faith. The mandalas used for contemplation in Hinduism and Buddhism are thought to bring the meditator to enlightenment if he or she can penetrate the depths of the symbolism.

The Sacred Mandala spread is adapted from the Mandala spread described in Rosemary Ellen Guiley's book, *The Mystical Tarot*, although many variations of spreads with the mandala theme exist. This particular spread is used as a tool for the contemplation of your inner reality. When used with the images of tarot, the mandala form can provide tremendous insight into the workings of your own psyche. As such, this spread is less well suited to forecasting the future than it is to developing self-knowledge and an understanding of your inner, spiritual life.

POSITION NUMBER ONE

The Self

The first card in the Sacred Mandala spread represents you, much like the significator in the Celtic Cross and Horoscope layouts. The difference here is that the first card in the Sacred Mandala spread signifies your self in a much broader, all-encompassing sense. The self here represents the totality of your being. This card is the foundation for the reading as it signifies you in the fullest sense.

POSITION NUMBER TWO

Ambitions, Desires

The second position in the Sacred Mandala spread signifies your desires in the most fundamental sense. It represents your instinctual urges and material cravings. As such, sexuality, lust, and desire for material benefit and the fulfillment of your basic needs are expressed here. Survival issues are also included in the influence of this position.

POSITION NUMBER THREE

Ideals and Aspirations

The third position reflects your deeper urges and desires. These can include your dreams and ideals and those things that offer you fulfillment in a more spiritual, humanitarian sense. This position is similar to the heart Chakra position and influences love, compassion, idealism, desires for accomplishment, and your overall well-being.

POSITION NUMBER FOUR

Actual Endeavors

This position influences those endeavors you actually choose to pursue in the real world, as opposed to the dreams and ideals that may or may not be expressed in action. This includes your career and the activities you pursue in your free time, such as hobbies, clubs, and organizations to which you belong. Comparing the influence of this position with that of your dreams can be quite revealing.

POSITION NUMBER FIVE

Dependencies, Addictions

This position reflects unhealthy attachments that impede your spiritual progress and the fulfillment of your dreams. False values and illusory comforts are among the attachments we form. These may include unhealthy desires for money, pleasure, or power. These attachments also include unhealthy relationships. Often this card indicates areas of our lives where a closer examination and reevaluation might produce the strength of will to let go of unhealthy attachments in order to form those that are beneficial to us.

POSITION NUMBER SIX

Strengths, Positive Characteristics

This position reveals your strong points, those qualities of character that are the best aspects of your personality. These assets distinguish you from others in a positive sense. Consider here how these positive traits are being utilized in your life and where they can be allowed to shine more powerfully by examining the relationship of this card to the others in the spread.

POSITION NUMBER SEVEN

Faults, Weaknesses

This position contradicts, or perhaps complements, the previous card. Here are your shortcomings and faults, those things in your life that need improvement. An honest look at this card in a spread can often reveal hidden weaknesses of which we may have been only partially aware.

POSITION NUMBER EIGHT

Self-Perception

This card reveals much about your own self-image, your perception and opinion of yourself. It can help you develop a realistic appraisal of yourself in light of your strengths, weaknesses, and overall tendencies and inclinations.

POSITION NUMBER NINE

Deepest Desire, Fulfillment

The ninth position is similar to the seventh card in the Chakra spread. This reflects your deepest desires; that which you believe would offer you the most fulfillment. This is the culminating card of the layout and integrates the meanings of the previous cards. In this card you can find insight into the higher purpose of your life.

TREE OF LIFE CARD LAYOUT

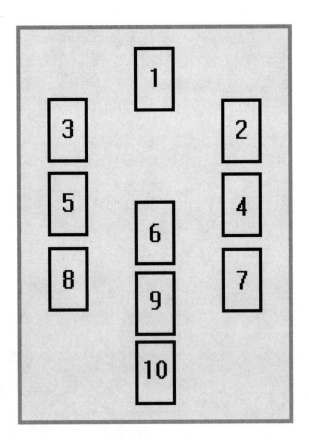

The Tree of Life spread is derived from the mystical tradition of the cabala. In cabalistic teachings, the Tree of Life consists of ten *sephiroth,* or spheres, which represent various stages in the mystic's ascent from the earth toward the glory of the One Divinity. The Tree of Life is, in a sense, very similar to the kundalini or chakra system of India in that it represents the path of ascent from the lowest levels of the material world to the highest levels of spirituality and experience of the godhead. However, the Tree of Life is also considered to be the means by which God descends from his glorious, heavenly realm into the world of humanity. The Tree of Life is therefore the link between God and man, as well as the means by which divinity and humanity are able to communicate and embrace each other.

Each position in this spread represents an aspect of the manifestation of the Divine Being. The top position, or crown, represents the highest level of spirituality, the dwelling place of God. The lowest position, or sovereignty, represents the world of matter in which human beings dwell. Yet despite the apparently tremendous gap between the world of matter and the world of spirit, the power of the divine can be known and experienced in each level. The Tree of Life is One, as God is One. The Divine Spirit permeates all levels of existence, from the lowest to the highest, and is accessible to all of us wherever we are in our journey along the Tree of Life.

This spread is perhaps the most complex tarot spread in that each *sephiroth* contains many levels of significance, far beyond the short interpretations given here. The *sephiroth* must also be considered in their relationship to one another. If you are interested in exploring this spread to its full depth, there are many books available that will help in your search to understand cabala further.

POSITION NUMBER ONE

The Crown

The crown position represents the highest level of divinity. It is the dwelling place of God in absolute, undifferentiated glory. Existing prior to the creation of all distinguished things, God dwells in perfect unity and oneness in the state of complete tranquility and potentiality. The crown position of the Tree of Life spread is analogous to the seventh chakra in the Chakra spread, representing the highest level of spiritual attainment possible, the ultimate union with the Divine Being.

Wisdom

The wisdom position of the Tree of Life represents the initial expression of the creative energy of oneness into the world of differentiated forms. It is the first sign of the transition from unity into duality, and from duality into multiplicity. The creation of the world is the expansion of the one into the many. Wisdom signifies intellect, rationality, and thought. In this sense, it contains the energy of strength, power, and rulership.

Understanding

Understanding is the complement of wisdom, and therefore represents the feminine aspect of duality. The feminine contains within it the powers of emotion, compassion, and love that provide balance and temperance to the strict intellect of wisdom. Just as wisdom may be considered to represent the masculine face of God, understanding represents God's feminine face. As the complement to wisdom, this position in the Tree of Life is another aspect of the duality that is represented in the yin and yang symbols and other dualistic images in mythological traditions.

POSITION NUMBER FOUR

Kindness, Mercy

The position representing kindness and mercy signifies the initial creation of the material world. "In the Beginning the earth was without form and void . . . and the Spirit of God moved over the waters." This is the story of the creation of the world, the beginning of the existence of manifested reality. This level corresponds most closely in our experience to creativity and the energy and motivation of new beginnings.

POSITION NUMBER FIVE

Judgment

Judgment is the complement to kindness and mercy and therefore represents the destructive energy of the world. The kindness and mercy position in the Tree of Life spread corresponds to Vishnu (the "sustainer") in the Hindu tradition. Judgment, on the other hand, corresponds to Shiva, the "destroyer." The world is a paradox of creation and destruction, life and death, positive and negative energies. However, the negative aspects should be considered as balancing, cleansing forces that prepare us for new experiences, rather than malicious forces seeking to destroy us.

POSITION NUMBER SIX

Beauty

The position of beauty represents the spirit, the greatest attribute of humanity and the human experience. Whereas the higher levels are somewhat more impersonal and transcendental, the level of beauty is intimately close to us as the primary link between God and humanity. This level represents the deepest aspect of your soul, the self in

Jungian terms, the atman of Hindu tradition. The figure of Christ is also symbolized in this position in that He represents the perfect union of flesh and spirit.

POSITION NUMBER SEVEN

Strength, Endurance

This position, despite a name that seems to imply traditionally masculine qualities, actually represents the realm of human emotions, intuition, love, and feelings. This position and the next (splendor, majesty) deal directly with elements of the human personality. In position number seven we are finally beginning to encounter the more concrete aspects of our experience as human beings. The higher levels are far more abstract in their meanings and tend to represent the cosmic elements of existence rather than the mundane.

POSITION NUMBER EIGHT

Splendor, Majesty

The eighth position on the Tree of Life represents reason and intellect, and therefore balances and complements the energy of the seventh position. Reason and intuition are complementary forces within us that must be balanced in order to provide us with power to live our lives well. The power of reason, if unchecked by a sensitivity to consequences and the feelings of others, may often lead us into situations or cause us to perform actions we may later regret. In the same manner, if we rely too exclusively on the strength of our feelings and emotions, we may be led into similarly troublesome situations. Reason and emotion must complement each other, and it is this balance that brings stability to our lives.

POSITION NUMBER NINE

Foundation

The foundation position represents our sexual energy center. However, in addition to physical sexuality, this position also influences the psychic energy underlying sexuality. In psychology, the concept of sublimation refers to the practice of redirecting sexual energy to other pursuits. In the Tantric tradition of Buddhism, sexual energy is often harnessed to bring the individual into higher states of consciousness. Sexuality is a very powerful force in our lives, above and beyond the mere physical expression of sex, and this power can be used to redirect our consciousness toward the spiritual.

POSITION NUMBER TEN

Sovereignty, Kingdom

The level of sovereignty is the energy center the primary influence of which is the material, physical level of our being. This circle of energy is most related to the primary issues of our bodies and the lower energies that pertain to fundamental concerns, such as basic physical survival. Of all the positions on the Tree of Life, sovereignty contains the lowest level of energy. However, despite its position as the lowest of the *sephiroth,* this level contains within it the full majesty of God just as all the other levels of the Tree do. God is present in all aspects of existence, and the potential to experience the divine is always within us.

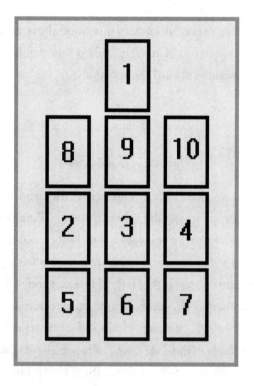

The Mystical Three spread utilizes the powerful symbolism of the number three to aid you in exploring your psyche. The number three contains significance on many levels and has been important in religious and mystical thought for millennia. In the Christian tradition, the number three is primarily significant in the concept of the Trinity: the one God existing in the three distinct yet unified personalities of Father, Son, and Holy Spirit. The number three appears in the symbology of the pyramids and in mandalas from around the world. Three also signifies the primary aspects of the human being: mind, body, and spirit. It is this triune aspect of humanity that is the focus of the Mystical Three layout. This spread is adapted from the spreads suggested in Rosemary Ellen Guiley's book, *The Mystical Tarot,* as well as Sergius Golowin's book, *The World of the Tarot.*

In this spread, there are three rows of three cards, representing mind, body, and spirit in the context of the three aspects of time: past, present, and future. The first card is revealed at the top of the three rows to represent the totality of the self, much like the significator in the Celtic Cross layout. Then the middle row, representing the present, is revealed. This is followed by the bottom row, the past, and then the top row, representing the future. When read from left to right, the vertical columns represent the body, mind, and spirit in ascending order. This layout offers insight into your personal development over time and provides an overview of your physical, mental, and spiritual well-being. Areas of personal strength and weakness are revealed by the symbolism in the cards, and you can use this knowledge to build on your strengths and work on those areas in need of improvement.

POSITION NUMBER ONE

The Self

The first card to be revealed is at the top of the spread and is known as the significator. This card represents your self in the most comprehensive sense. In this spread it should be seen as an umbrella encompassing the cards in the spread below it. This card covers the totality of the meanings gathered in the nine cards representing your mind, body, and spirit through time.

POSITION NUMBER TWO

The Body (Present)

The second card in this spread represents your current physical state. It may indicate positive or negative influences within and around your body, and offers a general overview of your physical condition in the present. Try to understand the general significance indicated by the card and don't read each image literally. The cards must be read in the context of the entire layout and an individual card is only a part of the overall impression offered by a spread.

POSITION NUMBER THREE

The Mind (Present)

This card represents your current psychological state. It reflects the thoughts, ideas, and emotions that currently dominate your mind or it may indicate areas of thought to which you have not given enough attention. If the card indicates turmoil or unease, you may need to be aware of areas in your life that are causing psychic stress so you can find ways to bring balance and tranquility.

POSITION NUMBER FOUR

The Spirit (Present)

This card represents your current spiritual state. This card should be considered thoughtfully for insight into your present spiritual life. You may find strengths you were overlooking or weaknesses you had forgotten about. This card offers the opportunity to take a spiritual inventory of our life at the present time.

POSITION NUMBER FIVE

The Body (Past)

The first card in the bottom row indicates the past state of your physical aspect. It may suggest to you areas in your life where you have experienced growth or healing in the transition from past to present. This card offers perspective on the card just above it, your present physical state. By examining the two cards in context of each other you can begin to understand the physical changes you have been through and the areas in which you have either progressed or moved backward.

POSITION NUMBER SIX

The Mind (Past)

This card should be read in context with the card just above it to get a perspective on the mental and psychic changes you have been through in the transition from the past to the present. This card can indicate areas of thought that had been predominant in your mind in the past and that may have been resolved. Often you will find areas in which you have grown or expanded your awareness when you compare the past and the present.

POSITION NUMBER SEVEN

The Spirit (Past)

This position represents your spiritual life in the past. Issues of change and growth apply to the comparison between this card and the one immediately above it. Spiritual struggles and issues in your past are also indicated.

POSITION NUMBER EIGHT

The Body (Future)

This position indicates areas of interest in terms of your physical life in the future. Issues of which you may be aware at present may continue to be important to you in the future, and this card indicates those trends. This card, like all the cards in the layout, must be read in the context of the entire spread. To get a full understanding of the implications in this position, you must observe the trends that were important in the transition from past to present, and project those trends into the future.

POSITION NUMBER NINE

The Mind (Future)

When taken in context with the two cards below it, this card indicates thoughts of interest or concern in the time ahead. Areas of present concern can often be carried into the future, and the future may also present opportunities to correct troublesome mental processes or to enhance beneficial ones. The future is not fixed and determined by the card indicated here. This position offers you insight into the directions you may want to take in terms of your intellectual life in the future and is a reflection of the things in which you are interested.

POSITION NUMBER TEN

The Spirit (Future)

This card indicates future directions you may want to take in your spiritual life. In addition, it may represent spiritual dimensions of your life that are or will be opening up in your consciousness as a consequence of your past and present spirituality. When read in sequence from past to present to future, this column of cards indicates the journey of your spirit through the world of matter.

PHILOSOPHY, PSYCHOLOGY, AND DIVINATION

What is Divination?

The word "divination" is derived from the Latin term *divinare*, which is literally translated into the verb "to divine." In typical usage, divination is thought of as the attempt to forecast the future through the interpretation of signs or messages from God, the gods, other spiritual beings, or perhaps from the future itself. These signs are sought in a multitude of places. Some examples of things that have been regarded as meaningful signs at various times in different cultures include the patterns of tea leaves in the bottoms of cups, the lines on the palms of the hands, the flight patterns of birds, the arrangement of entrails falling from the slaughtered bodies of sacrificial animals, the positions of the stars in the sky, and, of course, the interactions of groups of cards laid out in patterns or spreads. If we think of divination primarily in terms of the attempt to gaze into the future, we are confronted with two important questions. First, is it even possible to discern the future? And second, if it is possible, is it desirable for us to seek this kind of knowledge? These questions are important in our quest to understand the tarot because our answers to them will influence the attitude we bring to thinking the language of the cards.

Before attempting to answer these questions, however, perhaps we can explore a somewhat different understanding of divination if we consider the meaning of "divine" in and of itself. When we speak of the divine, we are generally speaking either directly about God (or the gods), or we are referring to attributes of the divinity such as omnipotence, omniscience, eternity, and so forth. One important attribute of the godhead (defined as the nature or essence of the divine) is omnipresence, which simply means the universal presence of the divinity in all things and in all places. It follows naturally that if God is omnipresent in this way, the all-pervading divine spirit resides within us as well. The idea that God dwells within the core of the human spirit is a key element in many systems of prayer and meditation, as well as numerous ethical and moral systems based on religious and mythological traditions. In addition, if we consider the divine to be eternal and therefore beyond the constraints of time as we perceive it, we could say that an aspect of divine consciousness is awareness of the future, since in the eternal mind the past, present, and future exist simultaneously and are not separate entities as we normally perceive them. From our perspective as time-bound humans, the future is a place in time that appears not yet to exist. From the vantage point of the godhead, however, all things are present and exist simultaneously. According to the teachings of nearly all religious or mythological traditions, divinity is not limited in any way by constraints, such as time and space, that confine the normal experience of humanity. The notion that God is the "all in all," existing far beyond our limited perception of time and space, opens up for us the possibility of a deeper understanding of divination than simply the effort to try to see into the future. If we define "to divine" as "seeking to know God or seeking to know the mind of divinity" instead of "seeking to know the future," then divination becomes a far richer source of wisdom, inspiration, and truth than our ordinary conception of it allows.

To accept that God is completely unhindered by time or space requires a radical shift in our normal conscious awareness of the universe. This view of the world forces us, if we take it at all seriously, to learn to see everything with which we come into contact as an extension of the divine nature of the godhead. In this sense, everything becomes sacred as an expression or emanation of the creative energy of God, and we learn to see the face of the divinity in all things. If the spirit of God dwells within all existing things, then all beings are therefore worthy of the greatest respect, and it is incumbent on us to treat each other with justice and equity. If the divine spirit is within us, we each have access to the wisdom of the divine mind.

The notion of the universally indwelling spirit of God is elegantly expressed in the Hindu belief in the atman. The atman is the deepest core of the individual human spirit, yet at the same time is an extension of the being of Brahma, the universal godhead. Imagine the fingers of a glove as individual entities or beings. Each finger of the glove superficially appears to have a unique and separate existence, yet the hand that fills the inside of the glove and gives each finger life and motion is really one indivisible unit. The being of the divine spirit can be conceived of in a similar way; each of us as individuals appears, like the fingers of the glove, to have a unique existence unrelated to that of any other individual. But at the deepest core of our spirit resides the unifying principle of the divine being, which is the source and sustainer of all existing things.

In Jungian terms, the deepest core of the individual spirit is called the self, which is conceptually similar to the idea of the atman. Although Jungian psychology does not necessarily accept or deny the existence of a divinity, the concept of Brahma, or the universal mind of

God, can be roughly equated to the collective unconscious in that it is a unifying storehouse of images and energy, available to all, that provides knowledge to us beyond the scope of the rational intellect. The collective unconscious is the repository of universally experienced archetypes and exists within each of us in much the same way as the atman dwells in each of us as the expression of Brahma. The archetypes provide us with the possibility of great knowledge because they collectively represent the vast experience of the entire human race from the very beginnings of human consciousness. However, the realm of the archetypes, or the atman, is normally hidden from our conscious awareness because we are conditioned to focus our energy on the external concerns of daily life and survival. The archetypes manifest themselves to us at times of crisis in our lives, or at times when we especially need guidance or important information in order to carry on. However, we cannot access them at will unless we are able to utilize some medium specifically designed to provide this access.

The tarot is just such a medium; its images, which are expressions of the archetypes, offer us the possibility of tapping directly into the wisdom of the self. As we learn to think in the language of the tarot, we increase our intuitive abilities and open our conscious awareness to the influence and perception of the archetypes. When we increase our ability to use intuition for guidance, we discover that our decisions and actions are much more in tune with our inner needs and desires, and we begin to experience greater emotional, spiritual, and psychological balance in our lives. We will also notice, as a consequence of more closely heeding the voice of our deepest self, that our future is shaped in accordance with those deepest desires and needs. As we move forward by paying close attention to the guidance of the spirit, we discover that specific questions or concerns about the future that may have caused us to seek predictions from divination will fall away in the proper expression of our true nature. If we think of divination as the act of seeking knowledge of the divine indwelling spirit, of the self, then we begin to realize the great power of synchronistic tools like the tarot to open up hidden vistas of insight that are eternally and universally available to us. Although the archetypal world resists being directly manipulated for our benefit, we can tap into its depths for guidance, and we can learn to use that wisdom for our benefit.

If we return to the two questions regarding the possibility and desirability of predicting the future, our new understanding of the process and meaning of divination may provide the answers we are seeking. Despite the fact that the mind of divinity is not bound by constricted notions of time, such as the past, present, or future; that an attribute of God is absolute timelessness; and that the divine spirit is universally available to all beings without the hindrance of spatial limitations, the concept of the divine in itself has little to do with directly forecasting the future. Yet if we accept these premises about the nature of divinity, the answer to our first question appears evident. If all aspects of what we call time are simultaneously and eternally present to the mind of God, then it is within the realm of possibility that the mind of the divine could pass that knowledge on to us in some way or other. The testimony of the various religious and mythological traditions of the world seems to bear out this possibility. In every religion and in every culture, prophets have arisen among the people to warn of impending catastrophes, and to call for a change in the culture and in the hearts of individuals in order to avert potential future disaster. Whether these prophecies were actual predictions or were written after the fact is not necessarily to the point. Rather, the important thing to keep in mind is that, to the mind prepared and willing to accept the existence of a divine spirit or a divine mind, things that seem out of the ordinary, or paradoxical to ordinary rational consciousness, may in fact be well within the parameters of acceptability. And if we are open to the possibility of a divinity that transcends time and space, certainly it is possible that such a being could communicate information to us about things that we are incapable of knowing directly.

Our discussion here is, of course, not constrained by the requirements of the scientific method, and I would not purport to have a scientific explanation for metaphysical phenomena. Yet even modern science bears out the possibility that knowledge of the future may be within the grasp of our minds. Modern theories of physics posit that the universe is far more chaotic and far more mysterious than the simple mechanics of Newtonian physics would lead us to believe. In the rational Newtonian perspective, cause and effect are clearly defined, clearly understood, and can be clearly perceived. However, in the bizarre cosmology revealed by Einstein's theory of relativity, phenomena that once seemed unthinkable to the scientific, rational worldview now seem not only possible, but in fact, even likely. If we consider the idea, for example, that time slows down considerably for someone who travels at the speed of light, we are immediately confronted with the difficult fact that time is not absolute and immutable, as was once thought. Because time and space do not have an absolute form and definition but are relative to our perceptions of them, there may be a rational explanation of possible communication from one place in time to another.

A tremendously fascinating discovery of quantum physics is that the behavior of certain subatomic particles changes by the very fact that they are being observed. This discovery appears to indicate that there is somehow an interaction taking place between the microcosmic world of the particles and the macrocosmic world of the human observer. If we think about the extraordinary behavior of these particles, we are forced to admit that our basic perceptions of the solidity and stability of the universe may be something of an illusion. This kind of causal interaction, which occurs without direct intervention on the part of the observer, strengthens the metaphysical notion that everything is interconnected and intimately related. If an observer of subatomic phenomena radically affects their behavior simply by observing them, then perhaps an individual who directly interacts with a deck of tarot cards can subconsciously influence their order of appearance in the course of a reading. The point here is not to get into a technical discussion of modern physics but rather to view these discoveries as a catalyst to open up perspectives that may help us understand the workings of the archetypal world of the tarot.

Divination versus Fortune-Telling

If the preceding discussions make sense in light of certain assumptions about the nature of the world and of reality, then it seems quite clear that it is possible for human beings to have access to information about the future. But we must consider whether having knowledge of the future is in fact desirable and beneficial. As was mentioned before, there are inherent dangers in having knowledge of the future. One obvious hazard is that because the future is not accessible to us in our ordinary states of consciousness, we may have incorrect information that could lead us into problematic situations. Since the images and signs "pointing" to the future require interpretation to be understood, the possibility that the interpretation of those signs is incorrect looms dangerously over us. Even if the prediction is correct in a general sense, the details may not be clear or may not be specifically accurate. If we understand divination to mean the attempt to forecast the future, it must be admitted that this practice is an art form and not by any means an exact science.

Suppose you have a tarot reading done for you, which predicts that within six months you will be starting your own business. The forecast indicates that you will be extremely successful in your new venture in a relatively short period of time and that financial prosperity will be yours at last. If you accept this prediction as truth, it is likely that for the next few months you will be on the lookout for any kind of interesting business opportunity. Now suppose that five months after the prediction you still have not started your business and are approached by someone with a business proposition that on the surface seems extremely exciting, almost certain to succeed. The initial investment seems reasonable, perhaps a few thousand dollars. Since you have convinced yourself that this must be the opportunity that was predicted for you, you proceed with the deal and invest the money. Of course, it may well be that this business opportunity becomes a tremendous success and you achieve the financial goals you have set for yourself. On the other hand, you may find that this business opportunity does not fit with your personality or your interests in any way. At first you struggle to put your full concentration into the venture, but then later discover that you are miserable in the work you must do to succeed in this business. Because of your lack of interest and motivation, the business begins to fail, and eventually you are forced to get out, taking a loss of the money you invested.

Despite the prediction, the success or failure of the business depends on your continued interest in it and your willingness to put forth the required effort to succeed. You alone are responsible for the ultimate outcome of this venture. If you jumped into the opportunity simply because you convinced yourself that the prediction was undeniably accurate, then you may have made the decision to enter that business venture on the basis of incorrect or limited information. After five months of waiting for the opportunity to appear, you assumed that the opportunity presented to you at the time must have been the business that was predicted for you. However, in your enthusiasm to fulfill the prediction, you may have overlooked a number of very important factors that should be considered when making such an important decision.

A careful consideration of whether the opportunity fits your personality and interests would certainly be a much better set of criteria on which to base this kind of decision than a prediction of your imminent business success. Perhaps the forecast for your future was correct in a general sense; the reader may have discovered that you have the type of personality that tends to start businesses and succeed in them. A better reading for you may have been to inform you of these apparent inclinations and offer guidance regarding methods of discovering the types of business for which you may be best suited. Certainly the reading should have been a catalyst for further exploration of your desires and the types of activities that you find appealing. The decision of whether or not to invest in this business would have been better made if you were armed with a greater degree of self-knowledge and insight and not simply a prediction of your imminent success.

At this point we should make a clear distinction between divination and fortune-telling. Divination should be considered in light of the discussions above as the effort to discover truth by seeking the divine wisdom of the self. Fortune-telling is defined as the attempt to discover one's fortune, which is the practice of forecasting the future. If we practice divination in a manner that aids us in developing our intuition and brings us greater knowledge about ourselves, then we will become wiser, more compassionate people. We will take responsibility for our own actions and our own future, and the decisions we make will be based on clarity of insight into our deepest inclinations and needs. Fortune-telling, by contrast, often distracts us from seeking knowledge of self because it promotes a false sense of security by leading us to assume that our decisions have already been made for us, that the future is immutable and out of our own control. Even if a prediction appears to have a negative outcome, there is still a sense of security gained from knowing (or believing we know) what lies before us. Feeling that our destiny is out of our own control may lead to a sense of powerlessness in which we feel unable to alter the course of our lives because of the sense that it has all been determined in advance by powers beyond our control. The danger of developing this sensibility of powerlessness is that it can induce an apathetic attitude in which we no longer take responsibility for our own destiny, actions, and decisions. Instead of helping us to grow as responsible individuals deeply aware of self, fortune-telling merely assists us in escaping from responsibility and self-knowledge. If practiced with the genuine desire to increase our wisdom and intimacy with self, divination can greatly assist us on the path toward personal enlightenment.

Freedom and Self-Determination

The philosophical question of free will versus predestination becomes an issue in any discussion of the tarot. The position throughout this book has consistently been that it is possible to have some knowledge of the future, but that the enlightened development of an individual's ability to exercise free will is preferable to the practice of seeking such knowledge. Yet an apparent contradiction exists in this position: If it is indeed possible for the future to be known, how can it also be possible that individuals possess the power of self-determination? If knowledge of the future already exists in the divine mind, then certainly the future must already be determined and therefore immutable. This issue is one of the thorniest philosophical problems known to mankind. It is important to acknowledge and explore these questions even if we're afraid of not having all the answers. One possible perspective to consider is that although free will and predetermination seem to be mutually exclusive, somehow they coexist in a paradox of epic proportions. Though this may not appear to be satisfying to the intellect, which demands clear distinctions and categories, there is something in this explanation that is satisfying to the heart. Most of us have had experiences of premonitions, or known of people who have had such experiences. Often these precognitive sensations are nothing more than hunches that something might happen in a certain way. Yet most of us also feel a clear sense that we are responsible for the choices that guide us through our day-to-day lives. Each morning we can choose whether or not to have a cup of coffee, whether to have oatmeal or bacon and eggs for breakfast, whether we'll go into the office or call in sick. We may not have the same grand perspective on the universe that the mind of divinity has, but we still sense that we have some destiny, some purpose to fulfill in our lives, be it great or small. Although the divine mind may know what choices we will make, it will never force us into a particular direction but leaves the actual decisions for us to make in absolute freedom. The paradox is that the choices may be known in advance, but they are still ours to make.

And why shouldn't this explanation be valid? Why can't apparently contradictory truths coexist? Jung spoke of the *coniunctio oppositorum,* the union of opposites, which is at the heart of the process of individuation, the process by which a person develops self-knowledge or enlightenment. Each of us is a mixed bag of good and evil, neurotic or destructive tendencies and powerful creativity, and reconciling these apparent contradictions is a key struggle in our effort to grow as mature individuals. The universe itself is a place of great mystery and paradox. Think again of the discoveries of modern physics: Time is relative and only seems to us to have substance and inviolability. Space can be curved, compressed, or completely ignored! Light itself is considered to be both wave and particle, which means that it is simultaneously a form of energy and a form of matter. An aspect of working with the tarot is the realization that the universe is a place of mystery, a magical kingdom in which contradictions can live together in peace, a place where the rational constructs of the human intellect have only limited validity, and in some cases may have no place at all. First and foremost, the tarot is a language of the soul. Deep within the unknown caverns of the unconscious there lies a world of wisdom and power, which will open itself to us if we are willing to put aside our ordinary conceptions and simply listen with an open mind.

THE CYBERTAROT EXPERIENCE

Why Using the CyberTarot Software Is as Powerful and Effective as Working with Real Cards

*M*ost people know the tarot as a deck of cards that is handled physically in order to do readings and divinations. Purists might argue that using a software version of the tarot is not as effective as using a real pack of cards because you are not actually interacting with the cards themselves, and therefore the cards are not able to absorb and reflect your personal energy. If the cards are devoid of your energies and your interactive input, the readings you receive from them may not be valid or accurate. A primary consideration in this regard is to define exactly what it means to interact with the cards and to transfer your energy into the cards so they can serve as an accurate reflection of your spiritual and psychological state. This interaction can be defined simply as the direct manipulation of the physical containers of the images of tarot, whether those containers are cards in your hand or the cards' images on a computer screen.

When you work with a physical deck of cards, you are continuously handling and manipulating the cards. You shuffle and rearrange the cards while thinking of your question, and continue to do so until you sense that the question has been answered. Then, you spread out the cards on a table and blindly select the ones you want to use for your reading. Finally, you turn the cards over in order to interpret their symbols. While you work with them, you may pick up individual cards to examine them more closely, or you may pick up a book or guide to help you understand those symbols. Another useful practice is to record your comments in a journal so that you can examine previous readings later, when you may have found additional insights to help you interpret them. All of these processes require some sort of direct interaction either with the cards themselves or with a notebook used to store information about your discoveries.

With CyberTarot you are able to interact with the card images in ways that are directly analogous to using physical cards. This software is unique in that it was designed from the ground up to work as accurately as possible and to allow you to work in the same way that you would with a tangible deck. After you set up your initial options in the software, you can shuffle the deck while you think of your question. The cards are actually shuffled for as long as you continue to hold down the **CTRL** key and the mouse button at the same time. In terms of the inner workings of the software, the cards that are displayed on your screen are actually being rearranged continuously until you release the **CTRL** key and the mouse button. The reason you are required to press both a key and a mouse button is to enable you to interact directly with the computer during the process of shuffling. By placing both hands on your computer in this way, you are in fact shuffling the cards with two hands, just as you would a real deck, and your energy is being transferred to the computer, just as it is transferred to the deck when you work with actual cards.

When you have completed shuffling, you select the cards you want for your spread from a fanned-out deck. Click your mouse on one of the cards, and while holding the mouse button, drag the card and drop it into the "pit" at the bottom of the screen. As you select the appropriate number of cards for your chosen spread, a miniature spread display indicates which positions you have filled. When you are finished selecting cards, the full-size view of the layout will be displayed. The software is designed to allow you, not the computer, to select the cards for your spread. The next step in working with the software is to "turn over" or reveal the cards. CyberTarot allows you to reveal cards one at a time or all at once. In either case, you can easily get information about a particular card or you can get a close-up view of the card. Not only is this similar to bringing a card closer to your eyes for better viewing, it is in fact more convenient because you can see the details of the card and read its interpretation at the same time without having to refer to a separate book for the information. Finally, you can quickly save readings with a complete set of your comments so you can refer to that particular reading again at any time. This feature allows you to save your observations about your readings as well as the readings themselves for easy access later.

CyberTarot is designed to enable you to use the medium of your computer as a direct means of interacting with the images of the tarot. The important thing to consider when deciding whether a tarot software program is as effective as an actual deck of cards is whether the reading experience offers you the occasion to interact with the symbols in a meaningful way. Tarot is symbolism, archetypes, and imagery much more than it is a stack of painted pieces of cardboard! Whether or not you are working directly with physical cards is irrele-

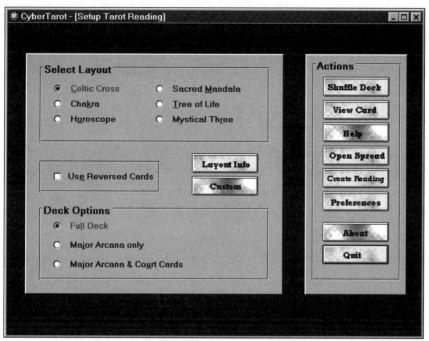

vant if the messages you receive in your readings are powerful and meaningful. Your clarity of intention when working with the symbols of the tarot are the true keys to the mysteries and truths about yourself that they can reveal. Reading the tarot successfully has much more to do with you and your interaction with the symbols than with the specific medium used to display the images.

Prepare for a Reading

The **Setup Tarot Reading** window is the main screen you see when you run the program. On this screen you can select any of the six available layouts, and you can set the option to enable or disable the use of reversed cards. From here you can also click **Shuffle Deck** to begin a reading, click **View Card** to view individual tarot cards one at a time, and get **Help** about how to run the software. **Open Spread** will let you open a reading you have saved before, and **Create Reading** lets you create your own reading by selecting the cards yourself. Finally, **About** has information about the software, and **Quit** will allow you to exit the software.

To begin using CyberTarot, select a layout from the options available in the **Select Layout** box on the **Setup** window. For information on the card layout you've chosen, click **Layout Info**. This will provide specific information on the card layouts available. CyberTarot offers three different layouts or spreads: the Celtic Cross, the Chakra, and the Horoscope.

Use Reversed Cards is enabled by default. You may disable the use of reversed cards by clicking the box to remove the **X**.

Once your setup options are complete, click **Shuffle Deck**. The cards will be spread out on the screen and a miniature layout will appear, along with a "pit" into which you will drag and drop the cards. Shuffle the cards by pressing the **CTRL** key and clicking on **Shuffle**.

Shuffling the Tarot Cards

When you hold down the **CTRL** key and click **Shuffle**, the cards will continue to be shuffled as long as you hold down both the **CTRL** key and the mouse button.

While you are shuffling the cards, think about the question or problem you wish the cards to help you understand more clearly. As you think about your question and shuffle the cards, your psychic energies will influence the cards to provide you with a reflection of your own instincts on the subject at hand. CyberTarot has a unique shuffling algorithm that actually continues to shuffle and rearrange the cards as long as you wish. In this way, the actual shuffling process is controlled by you, rather than by the computer. This process was designed specifically to allow you to shuffle the cards as you would shuffle a normal deck. In addition to the unique shuffling process, CyberTarot also allows you to select your own cards for your reading.

When you feel that you are ready to begin your reading, stop shuffling by letting go of the **CTRL** key and mouse button. A "pit" appears into which you can then drag and drop your selections. You will also notice that the cards are scattered unevenly so you can select any of the cards you wish for your reading. Each card you choose will be placed into the layout in the correct order. After you drop a card into the "pit," the card will fall into it and will then be placed in the proper position in the spread. Once all your cards have been selected, the layout will appear in full size on the screen and you can begin your reading.

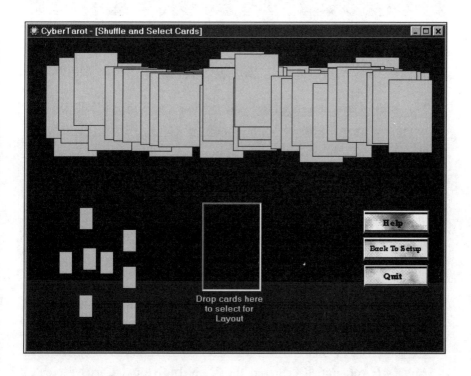

193

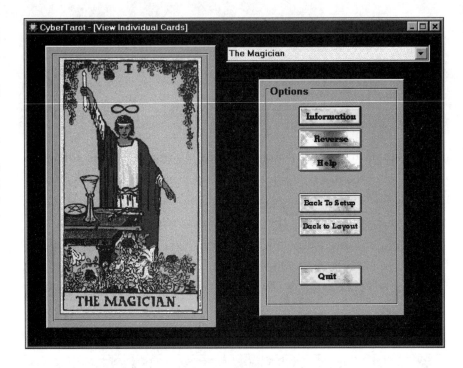

Viewing Individual Cards

The **View Card** screen allows you to view cards individually on a larger scale than is possible in the context of a layout. To view a particular card, click the arrow on the list box that appears above **Options** on the right side of the screen. The list will drop down and you will see the names of the cards. Use the scroll bar, the down-arrow key, or the page-down key to go through the names.

Once you select the card you want to view, it will automatically be displayed in the frame. If you want to get information about the meaning of the card, click **Information**. To reverse the image, click **Reverse**. The image will be flipped over. The **Interpretation** screen allows you to edit the interpretations and save your changes. Simply select any text you wish to change, type your own text, and click **Save**.

If you initially entered the **View Individual Cards** screen from the **Setup** window, you can return to **Setup** by clicking **Back to Setup**. If you were in the middle of a reading and wish to return to the reading, click **Back to Layout**. You can only return to the screen you were working on before you chose to view an individual card.

How to Work with a Spread

After shuffling and selecting cards, you will see the layout on a full screen with a **Control Panel** just to its right. The specific **Card Layout** or **Spread** screens allow you to work with a tarot spread in different ways, using the Control Panel and the right and left mouse buttons.

To begin the reading, click either **Reveal All** to display all the cards simultaneously or **Reveal One** to reveal one card at a time. The cards will be displayed in the spread. To get information about the

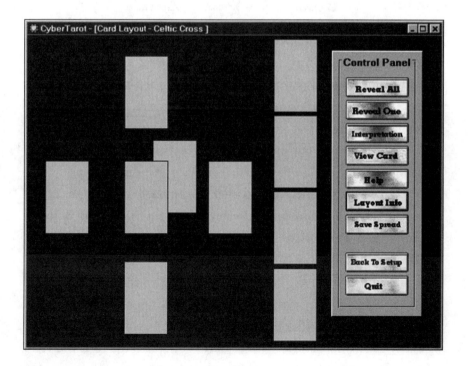

currently revealed card, either click **Interpretation**, or position the mouse pointer over the card you are interested in and click the right mouse button. When all cards have been revealed, **Interpretation** displays the interpretation for the entire reading. Information is also available about the spread you are working with by clicking **Layout Info**, and you can get a larger view of the current card by clicking **View Card** (only available if you are revealing one card at a time).

When all the cards in the spread have been "turned over," **Reveal** and **View Card** become disabled. To view a particular card on the View Card screen you can double-click that card with the left mouse button. To get back to the Layout screen from here, either double-click on the card image, or press **Back to Layout**. To simply get information about a particular card and its position on the **Layout** screen, click the card with the right mouse button.

Creating a New Reading Manually

You can set up a new reading manually using the **Create New Tarot Reading** screen. This screen allows you to select a spread and the cards you want to display in that spread. This may be useful if you do a reading using actual cards and want to save the information in your computer for later use.

To create your own reading, click **Create Reading** on the **Setup** screen to display the **Create New Tarot Reading** screen.

To set up the reading, click an option button to select a spread. Then, click on the card names you want to use from **Select Cards from This List**. As you select the cards, they will appear in **Cards to Be Displayed**. You will only be able to select the appropriate number of cards for the type of spread you have chosen. Once you have selected all the cards for the reading, you can modify the list of cards to be used by clicking on a card name to remove it from **To Be Used**. Then you can click **Select Cards** to replace the card you removed. If you want a particular card to be reversed, click the box to the left of that card's name in **Cards to Be Displayed**.

When you save or open the spread, the cards will be displayed in the order they are listed in **Cards to Be Displayed**. For example, if you use the Celtic Cross spread, the first card in the list will be the significator, the second card will be the crossing card, the third card will be the foundation, and so on.

Reading Interpretations in CyberTarot

If you click **On Top** on the **Interpretation** screen, the interpretation will stay on the screen as a "topmost" window. When you are on the **Layout** screen, you can get information about any single card by clicking the right mouse button on that card. You can double-click any card on a fully revealed layout screen to switch to the full card view screen for that card. To reverse the card image on the **View Individual Card** screen, click **Reverse**. To read the interpretation for the card currently shown, click **Interpretation**. To return to a layout either double-click the card image or click **Back to Layout**.

Technical Information

This section provides answers to some common technical questions about CyberTarot. Any questions not answered here may be answered at http://www.netcom.com/~edaviza.

Video Requirements

CyberTarot was designed and optimized to work at a minimum of 256 colors. If your display does not support a minimum of 256, colors of the tarot images will not be of satisfactory quality. In addition, a Windows optimized graphics display or accelerator card is highly recommended. If the images paint very slowly, or in "pieces" on the screen, it may be an indication that your video card and/or drivers may not support optimal graphics performance in the Windows environment.

"File Not Found" Error Message

CyberTarot consists of an executable file (**TAROT.EXE**), a help file (**TAROHELP.HLP**), various image files (extensions **.TRO** or **.TR_**), and the interpretation files (ending in extension **.DAT**). If any of the image files are missing you will encounter a message to reinstall the program. If you encounter a message stating that the **Help topic does not exist,** it means that the file **TAROHELP.HLP** is not installed or is in an incorrect directory. Reinstall the program onto your hard drive. All files should be installed into the same directory except the two files listed below.

"Could not find file VBRUN300.DLL or THREED.VBX" Error Messages

CyberTarot requires the dynamic-link library **VBRUN300.DLL** to be installed in the **\WINDOWS\SYSTEM** directory. The custom-control file **THREED.VBX** should be installed in this directory as well. If either of these files is missing, the program cannot be executed.

Saving a Tarot Spread on Disk

CyberTarot allows you to save your readings on disk to return to them at another time. The files are saved with the extension **.TRX** and can be saved to any directory, including floppy disks. The .TRX file is simply a text file containing information about the spread and the cards displayed, along with your personal comments about the reading. To open a saved spread, simply click the **Open Spread** button on the setup screen and select the spread you wish to read. If a .TRX file is corrupted and you attempt to open a spread with such a file, you will receive this error message: **The file you have selected either does not exist or is of an incorrect format.**

TAROT.INI Information File

The program automatically creates a settings file in its working directory called **TAROT.INI.** This file contains information about the window size and position of CyberTarot when you exit from the program so your screen size will be restored next time you run the program. It also contains information about the location of the program on your hard drive and your CD-ROM, as well as information about any custom spreads you may have created. The file is automatically backed up when you leave CyberTarot and is saved as **TARO_INI.BAK.** If your TAROT.INI file is lost or corrupted, you can simply rename **TARO_INI.BAK** to **TAROT.INI** to restore your most recently saved settings.

CPU and Memory Requirements

It is possible to run CyberTarot with a minimum 386 or compatible CPU. However, performance will be significantly improved by using a computer with a 486 chip, and we highly recommend a 486 or later chip for satisfactory performance. Your system should have at least 4MB RAM.

Windows Version Requirements

CyberTarot must be run in Windows version 3.1 or later, and will not run in Windows 3.0. Although CyberTarot is a 16-bit program, it works without any problems on Windows 95 and Windows NT.

Known Problems with Video Display Drivers

At the time of this release, there were problems with some older video display drivers from Headland Technologies and Diamond Computer Systems. Contact these manufacturers for information about possible upgrades or repairs to their display drivers if you are having difficulties running CyberTarot. With the Headland Technologies and Diamond Computer Systems drivers, a General Protection Fault may occur when attempting to shuffle the cards during a tarot reading.

Users of the Headland Technologies driver (HT256.DRV) can correct this problem by using a 256 color Video 7 display driver. These are usually included on the installation disks for Microsoft Windows 3.1. Run **Windows Setup** from the **MAIN** group in **Program Manager**, then select **Options, Change System Settings**. Select an option from the **Display** list, then restart Windows. You may need to install the drivers from the Windows installation disks if they are not already installed. If so, scroll to the bottom of the display list and select **Other Display**.

Users of Diamond Computer Systems Viper or Stealth cards have two options for correcting problems. First, using **Windows Setup** as above, select a display of 65,000 or more colors. The General Protection Fault usually only occurs when running at 256 colors. This may not work on your system if your graphics card does not have enough memory. The second option is to use one of Microsoft's generic 256-color Super VGA display drivers. These are available directly from Microsoft. You can also download these drivers from the Internet by searching the Microsoft Software Library at **http://www.microsoft.com** for **SVGA.EXE**. Some systems will already have the standard 256-color SVGA drivers installed.

APPENDIX A
GLOSSARY OF SYMBOLS

This glossary is provided to give you the basic definitions for a number of the words that commonly appear in the images of the tarot cards. The purpose of this section is not to provide a comprehensive symbol reference but to introduce you to some of the more ubiquitous images that appear in the tarot. For more detailed information on the meanings of specific symbols, or the history of symbolism in general, refer to the Bibliography for helpful and informative books.

Numbers

ZERO: the unmanifest, the beginning, emptiness, potentiality, yearning, the source

ONE: unity, divinity, completeness, godhead, the source of all, newness

TWO: duality, separation, conflict, potentiality, balance

THREE: creativity, fulfillment, the product of a union, the Trinity

FOUR: foundation, balance, perfection, solidity, stability, the four seasons

FIVE: the material world, humanity, the five senses, instability, distraction

SIX: health, restoration of balance, equilibrium, harmony

SEVEN: spirituality, mysticism, perfection, order, good fortune, luck

EIGHT: regeneration, stability, new life, eternity, the cycle of time

NINE: achievement, mysticism, fulfillment, truth, "three threes"

TEN: perfection, completion, the absolute, a return to the beginning, finality

Shapes

CIRCLE: cycles, repetition, time, rejuvenation, wholeness, completion, perfection

CROSS: union of heaven and earth, sacrifice, stability, union of opposites, similar to the square

LEMNISCATE: the number eight on its side; represents eternity, endless cycles, infinity

PYRAMID: four triangles with a square base, represents the earth's desire for the heavens, yearning, aspiration, union of matter and spirit

SQUARE: stability, earth, foundation, solidity, organization

TRIANGLE: Trinity, spirituality, upward movement, desire for the divine, aspiration

Colors

BLACK: emptiness, negativity, the void, destruction, dissolution

BLUE: water, coldness, clarity, rationality, spirituality, inspiration, the heavens

GOLD: perfection, power, completion, wealth, glory, beauty, divinity, the sun

GRAY: neutrality, depression, mourning, emptiness, penitence

GREEN: life, abundance, rejuvenation, springtime, freshness, fertility, youth

ORANGE: fire, potency, creative energy, love, emotions

PURPLE: royalty, majesty, pride, arrogance, justice, temperance, truth

RED: blood, life, life-force, danger, warning, fire, passion, strength, conflict, the sun

WHITE: purity, perfection, redemption, spirit, eternity, holiness

Individual Symbols, Objects

AIR: spirit, the heavens, intellect, rationality, coldness, the father archetype

BIRD: freedom, flight, creativity, thoughts, the spirit, aspiration

BUTTERFLY: the soul, liberty, freedom, transformation, rebirth, renewal, resurrection, joy

CADUCEUS: a staff with two snakes entwined around it; the symbol of medicine, healing, union of opposites, power, transcendence

CAT: night, the moon, darkness, stealth, cunning, secrecy, freedom, independence

CHILDREN: life, energy, youthfulness, newness, creation

CROWN: royalty, sovereignty, power, control, wisdom, victory, honor, reward

DOG: faithfulness, nobility, loyalty, companionship

EARTH: the material realm, heaviness, darkness, nurturing, the mother archetype, the soul, creativity

FIRE: power, energy, drive, forward motion, light, heat

FISH: life, fertility, procreation, water, renewal, a symbol of Christ

FRUIT: creativity, life, fruitfulness, productivity, joy, abundance

LILY: usually white, the lily represents innocence, purity, spirit

LION: the sun, fire, power, strength, majesty, glory, courage, perseverance, royalty

MOUNTAINS: the spirit, eternity, stillness, majesty, the heavenly realms

MOON: the unconscious, dreams, mystery, hidden knowledge, reflected light, illusion

OUROBOROS: a snake biting its own tail; represents the cycle of time, the godhead, unity, infinity, eternity, self-sufficiency, wisdom, immortality

ORB OR GLOBE: the world, majesty, dominion, sovereignty, power, wholeness, completeness

POMEGRANATE: symbol of Greek goddess Persephone, represents renewal, new beginnings, creativity, also the many forms of created reality because of its many seeds

RABBIT: the moon, lust, fertility, energy

RAINBOW: glory, the heavens, transformation, the spiritual realms, the link between heaven and earth

RAM: creative energy, potency, virility, power, the sun

ROSE: love, emotions, mysticism; red roses represent life, blood, sacrifice; white roses represent purity, spirituality

SALAMANDER: fire, faith, courage, bravery, energy

SCEPTER: divine power, royalty, dominion, authority, sovereignty, power

SNAKE OR SERPENT: wisdom, transformation, creative energy, resurrection, instinct, the life-force, temptation, darkness, duplicity

STARS: light, energy, the spirit, heavenly realms, illumination, clarity, the heavens

SUN: the godhead, divinity, the source of life, light, creativity, energy, power

SUNFLOWER: worship, magical power, longevity, spirituality, fruitfulness

TREE: life, link between heaven and earth, fertility, wisdom, shelter, protection, stability

WATER: creativity, emotions, receptiveness, life, nourishment, passivity

APPENDIX B
A SAMPLE READING USING ONLY
THE MAJOR ARCANA

This reading is an example that uses only the major arcana cards. Our sample will help you understand some of the differences between the major and the minor arcana and will give you the opportunity to see how to use only the major arcana cards in a reading. For our sample reading, let's assume the question is: "What is the most important interpersonal dynamic to consider in my current relationship?" Our spread contains the following cards:

Card One: THE HIGH PRIESTESS
Card Two: THE MOON
Card Three: TEMPERANCE
Card Four: THE HERMIT
Card Five: THE TOWER
Card Six: THE LOVERS
Card Seven: THE EMPRESS
Card Eight: THE CHARIOT
Card Nine: THE HIEROPHANT
Card Ten: THE HANGED MAN

The first card in the Celtic Cross spread represents you in the present time, and is known as the significator. The first card drawn in our example is the High Priestess. Our initial reaction may be one of surprise that a card such as the High Priestess appears as the significator in a reading about relationships. The High Priestess seems, at first glance, to represent an image of solitude and otherworldly spirituality. However, the High Priestess also indicates the union of opposing forces as represented by the two columns that flank her. The significance of the black and white columns is clear: In our reading, they represent the opposing forces of the partners in the relationship. Symbolically, a connection can be drawn with the Chinese philosophy of yin and yang: the black, female principle and the white, male principle. The High Priestess represents the union of these opposites, and therefore embodies a third element that is created by that union. Just as the chemical combination of sodium and chlorine produces salt, a new and radically different substance, so does the union of two individuals in a relationship produce a new substance, the relationship itself. The High Priestess appearing as the significator may indicate that the relationship is in need of a spiritual foundation that can strengthen the union of the opposite individuals involved.

The second card in the Celtic Cross spread represents important influences in your life and is known as the crossing card. These influences may be either positive or negative, internal or external. In our example, the crossing card is the Moon. The moon represents the unconscious and is an expression of your inclinations, instincts, and deepest desires. The theme of duality, the dynamic interaction of opposing forces, which was initially revealed in our significator, is repeated again in this card. In the distance we see two columns, which mirror the two columns in the card of the High Priestess. And in the foreground we see a dog and a wolf howling at the moon. The creature crawling from the water represents the hidden tendencies and disturbing images of our subconscious that occasionally appear in our dreams.

In the context of our question, we can consider the combination of the High Priestess and the Moon to be representative of the tension between the desire for independence and the desire to become more deeply involved in the relationship. Both cards express this conflict. The High Priestess is solitary, yet she clearly represents the union of opposing forces. As the significator, the High Priestess immediately suggests an answer to our question; perhaps the most important dynamic to consider in our current relationship is the tenuous balance between focus on the relationship and focus on ourself. The Moon, as the crossing card, more strongly indicates our own psychological and spiritual life, but there are symbols in the card that also express the interaction of opposites. Taken together, these two cards signify the necessity of balancing our energy between concentration on the relationship and investment in our own inner life.

The third card in the Celtic Cross spread is known as the foundation and represents the root issue that underlies our question. In our spread the card that appears as the foundation is Temperance. This card follows very logically upon the two preceding cards in that it offers a general sense of the need for balance and moderation in our lives. The Temperance card also contains images representing duality and the dynamic tension existing between the opposites. The angel pictured in the card holds two golden goblets, and her feet are resting alternately upon the land and the water before her. Again, the question we raised is reflected very clearly in this card. Temperance as the foundation reinforces the idea that the primary dynamic to consider in our relationship at this time is the need for balance.

The fourth card in the Celtic Cross spread is the card of the recent past. In our sample spread we have drawn the card of the Hermit. In the context of our reading, the Hermit seems to indicate a time in the past when we were not involved in a relationship, or a time during the course of the relationship when we may have been too preoccupied with our own concerns and interests to devote sufficient attention to our partner. The Hermit is a card of deep inner wisdom and self-sufficiency, and as such seems to contradict the trend of the previous three cards in which solitary energy is balanced with the energy of union. Perhaps the reading is indicating that our present concern about the most important dynamic of the relationship is a healthy step away from a previously self-centered attitude about the relationship. Or, the Hermit may represent a solitary past that is being significantly altered by the growth of a relationship. The psychological change involved in moving from a solitary life to a life in a relationship is often difficult to bear, and the tensions created by this change can be very challenging. The cards are indicating the need for balance and wisdom during what may be a difficult transition.

The fifth card in the Celtic Cross Spread is the crowning card and represents issues of concern in the transition between the present and the future. The crown in our sample spread is the Tower, which seems to indicate destruction and collapse. However, this card does not necessarily indicate that the relationship will fall apart at some point in the future. It is important to remember that the cards should not be taken literally or at face value, but that a deeper meaning should be sought in the context of the entire reading. Perhaps this card, in our current context, is indicative of our own fears or worries about the future of the relationship. If we have approached the tarot with a specific question about our relationship, clearly we have some concern about the nature or stability of the relationship. The Tower in the position of the crown in our reading may simply reflect the concerns we have about the future of the relationship. Alternately, the Tower may be a reminder to work on maintaining the balance indicated in the card of the foundation in order to prevent the dissolution of the relationship.

The sixth card in the Celtic Cross spread represents the future. In our example spread, the card of the Lovers appears in this position. The indications of this card seem clear. An angel hovers over the couple and offers a blessing on them. The general mood of the card is peace, satisfaction, and fulfillment. In the context of the overall reading, the card of the Lovers indicates the possibility of a happy relationship over time, if we are able to maintain the balance indicated by earlier cards in the spread. Of course, this card should not be taken literally as a predetermined and certain future, but rather as an indicator of possible future trends. The card of the Lovers offers a number of interesting parallels with the significator in our reading. The image of the High Priestess is that of an individual person who sits between two columns. In the Lovers, two people are depicted, and between them is a mountain peak. The contrast of these cards indicates that there has been a change of focus from the individual (the High Priestess), to the united couple (the Lovers). The trend of the reading thus far indicates that a positive future is possible if a balance is developed and maintained between our needs and the needs of our partner and of the relationship.

The seventh card in the Celtic Cross spread concerns emotions and feelings. In our reading the Empress has been drawn as the card of emotions. The Empress is a very powerful archetype of motherhood, and thus represents caring, nurturing, and attentiveness. The Empress provides a complement to the High Priestess as our significator. Both images depict a solitary woman, yet while the High Priestess represents the spiritual, inner life of an individual, the Empress represents the external, more public life of that individual. In our reading, the High Priestess indicates the tension between a solitary life and a life lived in the context of a relationship. The crux of her meaning centers on our own concerns about the relationship at the present time.

The Empress, as an archetype of nurturing, represents the need for an emotional investment in the relationship in order to fulfill its potential. This card clearly bears significance as an expression of our emotional state at the time of the reading. When interpreted in context of the whole reading thus far, the Empress indicates that our concerns at present revolve around the emotional energy necessary for the relationship. The Empress reminds us here that significant emotional energy and a great deal of care must be invested to build a lasting relationship. She also reminds us to balance the nurturing of the relationship with the care of our own soul.

The eighth card of the Celtic Cross spread signifies the influence of others in our lives. In our reading, the "others" indicated by this position may simply be our partner in the relationship. The Chariot bears out this interpretation. The theme of duality, the tension between the opposites which we saw in a number of earlier cards, is very clearly manifested in the image of the Chariot. The charioteer in our image is a symbol of strength and the determination required to maintain the balance between opposing forces, represented here by the two sphinxes pulling the chariot. In the context of our question, this card may represent the determination of our partner to maintain and build the relationship. If this is not clear from our current situation, the card of the Chariot may be prompting us to look not only within ourselves for information about the relationship, but also at our partner's current feelings about the relationship. A relationship requires balance and effort on the part of both partners, and without a consensus and the determination of both individuals to work together, it will not endure the challenges of the long term.

The ninth card represents our hopes and desires for the outcome of the question we have brought to the tarot. The Hierophant offers parallels with nearly all of the previously drawn cards in our reading. Like the High Priestess, the image depicts a solitary individual, representing our spiritual life, flanked by two columns. In the Hierophant, however, there is the added element of the two people standing at the feet of the spiritual leader. The motif of a single element flanked by two contrasting elements has been consistently displayed in many of the cards in our reading. The consistent theme is that of the tension between the interests of the individuals involved and the interests of the partnership. The Hierophant, for the first time, offers the image of a person flanked not only by inanimate stone columns but also by other people. As the expression of our hopes for the outcome of the current situation, the Hierophant seems to indicate that our desire is, in fact, to find the appropriate balance to sustain not only the relationship but also our own individuality.

The tenth and final card in the Celtic Cross spread represents the culmination or the final outcome of our question. For this card we have drawn the Hanged Man. The Hanged Man seems to present a stark contrast with the previous cards we have drawn in our spread. In most of the previous cards, the image of duality and tension between opposing forces was a primary concern. The image of a single individual in the Hanged Man brings the focus of the reading back to ourselves as individuals. Our question for this reading related to the dynamics involved in our current relationship, yet as the culmination we have drawn a card that signifies the sacrifice offered by an individual. This image offers a fitting close to our reading in that it indicates the need of the individuals in the relationship to make personal sacrifices occasionally in order to strengthen and sustain the relationship.

The message of the reading as a whole offers us the suggestion that the most important dynamic in our relationship at the current time is the struggle to find balance between protecting the interests of the individuals and protecting the interests of the partnership. In order for the relationship to continue and remain healthy, the partners must strive to find a balance between self-interest and self-sacrifice. The challenge is to remember the importance of this tension and to find creative ways to sustain and maintain the balance between these opposing concerns.

BIBLIOGRAPHY

The following are important books that will help you in your understanding not only of the tarot but also mythology, symbolism, and the workings of intuition and the psyche.

Arya, Usharbudh. *Philosophy of Hatha Yoga*. Honesdale, Penn.: The Himalayan Institute of Yoga Science and Philosophy of the U.S.A., 1985.

Campbell, Joseph. *The Hero with a Thousand Faces*. Princeton, N.J.: Princeton University Press, 1968.

———. *The Mythic Image*. Princeton, NJ: Princeton University Press, 1974.

———. *Myths to Live By*. New York: Bantam Books, 1973.

Cooper, J. C. *An Illustrated Encyclopaedia of Traditional Symbols*. New York: Thames and Hudson, 1979.

Eliade, Mircea. *Patterns in Comparative Religion*. New York: Meridian Books, 1958.

——. *The Sacred and the Profane.* New York: Harcourt Brace Jovanovich, 1987.

Epstein, Perle. *Kabbalah: The Way of the Jewish Mystic.* Boston: Shambhala Publications, 1978.

Giles, Cynthia. *The Tarot: History, Mystery, and Lore.* New York: Paragon House, 1992.

Golowin, Sergius. *The World of the Tarot.* York Beach, Maine: Samuel Weiser, 1988.

Grey, Eden. *Mastering the Tarot: Basic Lessons in an Ancient, Mystic Art.* New York: Penguin Books, 1988.

——. *The Tarot Revealed.* New York: Penguin Books, 1988.

Guiley, Rosemary Ellen. *The Mystical Tarot.* New York: Penguin Books, 1991.

Jung, Carl G. *Memories, Dreams, Reflections.* Recorded and edited by Aniela Jaffe. New York: Vintage Books, 1965.

Kaplan, Stuart R. *The Encyclopedia of Tarot.* New York: U.S. Games Systems, 1978.

Nichols, Sallie. *Jung and Tarot: An Archetypal Journey.* York Beach, Maine: Samuel Weiser, 1980.

Sharman-Burke, Juliet, and Greene, Liz. *The Mythic Tarot: A New Approach to the Tarot Cards.* New York: Fireside, 1986.

Talbot, Michael. *The Holographic Universe.* New York: HarperCollins Publishers, 1992.

Waite, Arthur Edward. *The Pictorial Key to the Tarot.* Secaucus, N.J.: Citadel Press, 1959.

Wang, Robert. *The Qabalistic Tarot.* York Beach, Maine: Samuel Weiser, 1983.

Woolfolk, Joanna Martine. *The Only Astrology Book You'll Ever Need.* Chelsea, Mich.: Scarborough House, 1990.

ABOUT CYBERTAROT

CyberTarot was conceived, written, and developed by Edward A. Aviza. The card sound effects, and the "Reveal All" theme in Cyber-Tarot are composed and performed by Michael DiSilvestro. Mr. DiSilvestro has studied music composition and performance for more than fifteen years. He has a degree in business administration and currently resides in the Chicago area. He is actively involved in creating musical scores for multimedia software.

For further information, visit Edward A. Aviza's home page at http://www.netcom.com/~edaviza.

CyberTarot was produced by Jaqueline Lightfield.

The voice narration in CyberTarot is by Jaqueline Lightfield. Musical accompaniment to voice readings and introductory theme music are by Harry J. Williams, Equinox Music.

The Mythic Tarot, with text by Juliet Sharman-Burke and Liz Greene and illustrations by Tricia Newell, is edited, designed, and printed by Eddison Sadd Editions, St. Chad's Court, 146b King's Cross Road, London WC1X 9DH, and is copyright © Eddison Sadd Editions 1986. No reproduction of the text or images from *The Mythic Tarot* may be made without prior permission in writing from Eddison Sadd Editions.

The Mythic Tarot is published around the world by various publishers and should be available from all good bookshops, or directly from the publisher. In some countries, *The Mythic Tarot* book and The Mythic Tarot deck are available separately, along with *The Mythic Tarot Workbook.* Please contact the publishers directly for further details or Eddison Sadd Editions. The publishers are:

Australia:	SIMON & SCHUSTER AUSTRALIA
Brazil:	LIBRARIAS SICILIANO
Canada:	STODDART PUBLISHING
France:	EDITIONS SOLAR
Germany:	HEINRICH HUGENDUBEL VERLAG
Italy:	ARMENIA EDITORE
Spain:	EDITORIAL EDAF SA
UK:	RANDOM HOUSE UK
U.S.:	SIMON & SCHUSTER

ABOUT THE AUTHOR

Edward A. Aviza has a degree in Philosophy and Religious Studies from the University of Illinois at Urbana-Champaign. He is currently employed as a technical analyst in the Chicago area. His grandparents introduced him to the tarot when he was fifteen, teaching him to interpret the images from a Jungian perspective. Mr. Aviza studied fiction writing at Columbia College, Chicago, as well as in independent workshops. He lives in the Chicago area with his wife Dale, their son Austin, and two cats, Weebles and Ellie Mae.